Arguing with Socrates

ALSO AVAILABLE FROM BLOOMSBURY

The Bloomsbury Companion to Socrates, edited by John Bussanich and Nicholas D. Smith
Plato: A Guide for the Perplexed, Gerald A. Press
Plato's Republic, Luke Purshouse
Socrates: A Guide for the Perplexed, Sara Ahbel-Rappe

Arguing with Socrates

An Introduction to Plato's Shorter Dialogues

CHRISTOPHER WARNE

BLOOMSBURY
LONDON • NEW DELHI • NEW YORK • SYDNEY

Bloomsbury Academic
An imprint of Bloomsbury Publishing Plc

50 Bedford Square
London
WC1B 3DP
UK

175 Fifth Avenue
New York
NY 10010
USA

www.bloomsbury.com

First published 2013

British Library Cataloguing in Publication Data
A catalogue record for this book is available from the British Library.

ISBN: HB: 978-1-4411-8717-8
PB: 978-1-4411-9544-9
ePub: 978-1-6235-6991-4
ePDF: 978-1-6235-6254-0

Library of Congress Cataloging-in-Publication Data
A catalog record for this book is available from the Library of Congress.

Typeset by Fakenham Prepress Solutions, Fakenham, Norfolk NR21 8NN
Printed and bound in India

To Cathy

Thank you

CONTENTS

PREFACE

When I first studied Plato at university and consulted the secondary literature, I quickly found myself immersed in established scholarly debates that did not always meet my needs as a second-year undergraduate. Frequently, arguments appeared to have been plucked from dialogues and appraised with reference to remarks in other dialogues, which left little sense of whole from which they were taken. Many years later I returned to Plato and was fascinated by the stories and the themes of the individual dialogues. There is, of course, much to learn from scholarly debate, and this book, like many others, owes a great deal to the careful work of commentators and philosophers. However, I realised that the scholarly arguments were not the best place to begin one's reflection on the material.

The first part of this book contains some general reflections about the dramatic and philosophical aspect of the shorter dialogues. The second part comprises a series of essays each devoted to a particular dialogue. Each essay begins with a discussion of the drama of the dialogue in question and then moves on to some reflections on the, or in the case of longer dialogues a, primary theme. I have attempted to conduct these discussions without any reference to Plato at all. Some of the claims developed in those sections are controversial. That is a deliberate attempt to stimulate the reader before engaging with the views of Socrates' interlocutors.

Several friends have helped me in the writing of this book. Their expertise, insight and enthusiasm have consistently impressed and energised me. In particular I thank Nick Dent, Rob Hopkins, Iain Law, Jon Phelan, Beccy Simpson, Chris Wraight and Tom Humphrey. They have commented on draft material and discussed with me some of the issues that appear in the book. Sarah Campbell and Rachel Eisenhauer at Bloomsbury have shown both support and much valued patience.

I am very grateful to my family for their support in recent years. The subject matter of this book is remote from their everyday concerns, but all have taken an interest in a desire to help me complete the project. I am especially indebted to my parents who, at a late stage, turned over a room in their house to me to use as an office.

This book is dedicated to my wife, Cathy. She encouraged and supported me in this project and has had to bear more than her fair share of our domestic responsibilities during the time of its completion. In thought, word and deed she shares in the authorship of the book. Our four-year-old son, Alfred, entered my study a few months ago to find the printer spewing pages and pages of typescript on to the floor. 'Daddy,' he asked, 'why do you need so many words?' It was a fair point and I only hope the reader doesn't too readily come to share his scepticism. Our two-year-old daughter, Lucy, was sitting on my lap earlier on today as I closed the lid of the computer. 'Fank you,' she quipped. And gratitude seems a fitting note on which to end. Fank you too.

Christopher Warne
Walton-on-Thames
25 September 2012

PART ONE

CHAPTER ONE

People

Introduction

The purpose of this chapter is to say something, necessarily brief, about the people of Plato. Such an undertaking may seem at odds with the principal matter at hand, which is the study of philosophy. But the form of Plato's writings presents the reader with a problem.[1] Although they are possibly the most famous works of philosophy in the Western canon, they are formally dialogues as opposed to conventional treatises. Our desire to delineate Plato's philosophy makes it tempting to treat the dialogue form as detachable and dispensable, as if Plato had intended to write disguised treatises.[2] If we succumb to that temptation it becomes equally tempting to think that Plato expresses his views[3] through the mouth of the main speaker, Socrates. Privileging the contribution of Socrates in this way reduces the significance of the interlocutors, who quickly become mere voices for the prejudices and views Plato wishes to challenge. One of the motivating thoughts behind this book is that this is a mistake. The interlocutors are more than one-dimensional foils for Socrates' philosophising, and part of Plato's meaning is, I think, lost to us if we treat them as such.[4]

There are, of course, famously different readings of Plato's works. Some scholars argue for a unitarian reading, the central claim of which is that all the dialogues ascribed to Plato are expressive of a single point of view. Opposed to that are various developmental readings, which divide the corpus into early, middle and late dialogues. Participation in that debate, however, is posterior to a close and impartial reading of the dialogues themselves. Thus the essays in Part Two emphasise the people and the drama of Plato with a view to assisting the reader and preparing them for the debates in the secondary literature.

The salient biographical details of the interlocutors will emerge in our discussion of the individual dialogues themselves. In this chapter I shall simply raise one or two very general points with a view to correcting our tendency to concentrate our attention on Socrates' contribution.[5] Readers with an interest in our historical knowledge hereabouts should consult the volumes detailed in the notes.[6] All fifth- and fourth-century dates in the text are BC.

Socrates

Scholars rightly preface their comments about the life of Socrates with some cautionary remarks about the 'Socratic Problem'. This is the problem of distinguishing the historical Socrates from the Socrates represented in the classical literature. There are three principal biographical sources: Aristophanes, Xenophon and Plato. The first is accusatory, the other two defensive: all three, superficially at least, are inconsistent with one another. To exaggerate the contrast a bit: Aristophanes' Socrates is a natural scientist; Xenophon's a purveyor of bland avuncular advice; and Plato's a philosophical sceptic. The only indication we have that Socrates himself wrote anything that might possibly lend weight to one or other source is the comment in the *Phaedo* that he wrote poetry during his final days in prison (60cff.). Any such poetry has not survived and, other than neatly offending the conventional wisdom that 'Socrates, like Jesus, wrote *nothing*', the remark in no way delivers us from the quandary: who was the historical Socrates?

This is not the place, and this is not the author, to lock horns with the problem.[7] The matter is vexing and the prospects for a satisfactory resolution are dim. Indeed one recent biographer writes, rather dispiritingly, that 'the historical Socrates is pretty irrecoverable'.[8] I mention the problem only to set it aside: our concern is Socrates the character in Plato's shorter dialogues and not Socrates the man. The comments that follow are limited to that representation.[9]

Socrates was born in 469 in a district south west of Athens and was executed in 399 for impiety and corrupting the young. Plato's dramatic portrait of Socrates spans the period from c. 450 (*Parmenides*) to 399 (*Phaedo*): from the Golden Age of Pericles through the long, terrible Peloponnesian War to the aftermath of the fall of Athens in 404. The story is a sad one: a decent man watches the demise of the city he loves only to be convicted of having contributed to its downfall.[10]

Although Socrates loved Athens, he was far from a conventional citizen. The Athenians prized beauty, wealth and political power. Socrates was ugly, poor and went out of his way to avoid public office.[11] Accounts of his early life and occupation are speculative: for instance, he may have studied with the natural scientist Anaxagoras and possibly worked as a mason or usurer. What is reasonably clear, however, is that he earned his distinction among the Athenians for his war record and later for his being a terrifically annoying busybody. Unfortunately, the significance of neither point is wholly straightforward. Although he was by all accounts a brave soldier, he excelled himself in *retreat*.[12] He was also responsible for saving the life of Alcibiades, a controversial figure who would later betray the Athenians. Then there was the matter of his being a busybody: Socrates cheerfully characterised himself as a gadfly at his trial, a clear acknowledgement of the irritation he visited upon his fellow citizens. But, he maintained, he had done this at Apollo's behest and out of a genuine concern for the souls of the Athenians.

The single most arresting detail of his life remains his trial and subsequent execution in 399. Although he had been an object of public attention for at least a quarter of a century before then, events came to a head in 404–3. Having suffered defeat at the hands of the Spartans, Athens was governed by The Thirty: men with pro-Spartan sympathies whose bloody rule is notorious. Many democrats were killed; many more fled and staged an uprising in 403. Socrates, however, did not flee. He was furthermore closely associated with Critias and Charmides, two prominent members of The Thirty. In the aftermath of the civil war, Socrates' former quirkiness looked more like subversion. Here was a man who influenced The Thirty and was perceived to be the educator of Alcibiades. In the *Meno* Plato represents Socrates after the restoration of democracy continuing his practice of question and answer right under the nose of Anytus, the man historically thought to be behind his prosecution (89eff.). He was finally indicted by Meletus and found guilty by a small majority. However, far from silencing the gadfly, the execution of Socrates cemented his place in history and made of him a martyr for philosophy.

Today Socrates enjoys the status of a hero and there is a tendency among readers to think of him as one of us.[13] But he was obviously a controversial and divisive figure: he upset a lot of people and may have made a bad situation in Athens worse. There is, I think, much more to learn from these dialogues if we resist the temptation to think of Socrates as espousing of the views of a modern liberal academic. For example, from time to time Socrates says some fairly outrageous things. In the *Crito* he argues that citizens owe an absolute obedience to the state (51bff.). This is not a view we share today. But the desire to domesticate Socrates, to make him a modern liberal who stands shoulder to shoulder with us, often results in more or less implausible efforts to argue that what he said is not what he actually meant. So we finesse such remarks or dismiss them altogether as instances of his famous irony. But in so doing we disarm the most important question of all: Do we, *could* we, owe an absolute obedience to the state?

As it happens, there are, I think, aspects of Plato's portrait of Socrates that might make us think twice about wishing to befriend him so readily. In the first instance, Socrates was a bit of a bully. He professes genuine solicitude for the Athenians (*Apology* 29e), but he frequently orchestrates their public humiliation. It's worth contrasting this with his views about the proper treatment of wrongdoers, who, he says, should be taken aside and privately disabused of their ignorance (*Apology* 26a).

Then there is the scope of Socrates' inquiry: nothing, it seems, should be taken for granted. He targets what every good Athenian knows: the nature of bravery, justice and excellence. We should not, though, pretend that Socrates would spare our most cherished attitudes. Take, for example, our commitment to racial equality. In the popular media, that commitment is seldom subjected to the kind of patient scrutiny Socrates is apt to bring to bear on bravery or justice. There was, for example, public outcry in 2009 when Nick Griffin, the leader of the British National Party, was invited to speak on a platform with members of other political parties for the BBC's programme *Question Time*. Although the event ultimately galvanised the wider community's opposition to racism, his presence was felt to be offensive by members of the public. Think also, in this connection, of the alarmingly hostile reaction to Peter Singer's appointment to Princeton in 1999. Even his mildly controversial discussion of the sanctity of life prompted large and vilifying protests.[14] The point is not, of course, that the public's reaction to a philosopher constitutes an index for the value of his work. It is simply that we should not think for one minute that our admiration for Socrates' philosophical ability would prevent him from subjecting us, and our beliefs, to his critical practice.

Naturally, there is much to be said in reply to these points. Socrates' bullying, for example, can be reinterpreted as a case of 'tough love', and his willingness to question conventional wisdom can be presented as the true posture of the dispassionate scientist. But such replies really serve to confirm the underlying point I have tried to make: the appraisal of Socrates is *disputable*. We should, I recommend, cultivate a healthy scepticism towards the character and the arguments he makes in Plato.

The interlocutors

If we have a tendency to venerate Socrates we have an equal tendency to denigrate his interlocutors. This is perhaps unsurprising: these men are traditionally held to be the repositories of some fairly hopeless views about bravery, justice and piety.[15] Furthermore their conversations with Socrates end in *aporia* (literally, an impasse) and that encourages the thought that their views are philosophically uninteresting. But we must be careful to avoid exaggeration hereabouts, and for two reasons.

First, neither their views nor their argumentative powers are uniformly bad. Take, for example, Meno's first answer to the question 'What is virtue?' He lists the virtue of a man, a woman, a child and so on (71e–72a). His answer fails because he has not specified that common property the presence of which makes them all instances of virtue. But if we do this on his behalf we can see that he conceives of virtue as a matter of each doing his own job. This is the account of justice Socrates spells out in the *Republic* and there takes perfectly seriously (433a–b).[16]

Second, in a surprising number of cases the interlocutors state views that remain popular today. We may smile condescendingly when Euthyphro stresses the threat of miasma as a result of what he perceives to be his father's impiety because we don't believe in the idea of spiritual pollution (4c). But we are just as wary of guilt by association: relatives and friends of disgraced people sometimes distance themselves from them in the press to remove the slightest suggestion that they might endorse the misdeeds. We may likewise not think much of Laches' definition of bravery as simply not leaving one's post (190e). But something like that conception of bravery was sufficient for the world press to condemn Francesco Schettino, the captain of the *Costa Concordia*, as a coward in 2012.

This is not to say that the interlocutors' views are, contrary to Socrates' assessment, philosophically robust. We don't, for example, think Laches has identified the property that explains the bravery of all brave actions (and nor does he for that matter). The point is simply that we may have more in common with the interlocutors' way of thinking about these matters than we care to believe and that this should inform the way we read them.

One group of interlocutors, though, does deserve further comment. People ended up in conversation with Socrates because they professed to know something about the world. In the *Apology* Socrates identifies three classes of such people: politicians, poets and artisans (21cff.). When we survey the Platonic corpus, however, we have cause to doubt the accuracy of this statement: for though Socrates does talk to some politicians, we do not find him in conversation with poets, nor with artisans. In fact, in many instances we find him in discussion with sophists.[17]

Despite their not appearing on Socrates' list of interviewees, the sophists plainly fall within his remit: after all, they profess to know something sufficiently well to present themselves as teachers and to collect large fees for their services. The term 'sophist' is nowadays somewhat derisory and these men emerge as something like the villains of the Platonic corpus. Traditionally, Plato is thought to have harboured a real enmity towards the sophists: part of his motivation in writing, according to some commentators, was his desire to cleave a line between them and Socrates.[18]

But the traditional view is misleading, as George Kerferd's excellent and beautifully written study demonstrates. They *were* wise men. For example, we owe to Hippias of Elis, whom scholars allege Plato represents as a buffoon, our ability to date events in the ancient world. He further retains the credit for having discovered the quadratrix, a curve used in certain geometrical constructions.[19] Socrates, however, does not dispute the sophists' claim to know about mathematics or history; he is solely concerned with their claim to know the nature of virtue and to teach it. Unlike the Athenians he doesn't seem to have been disturbed by the principle of charging fees nor the sophists' lack of discrimination with regard to whom they taught.[20]

But it's also not even entirely clear that Plato thought the sophists constituted the opposition in this drama. Take, for example, the simile of the large and powerful animal in the *Republic* (493aff.). Socrates compares the sophists to a man in charge of a wild beast. The man becomes an expert observer of the animal's nature: he knows what it wants and what its behaviour means. But he does not know which of the creature's predilections is noble or base. The same is true of the sophists, who are little more than close observers of human preferences. The sophists do not influence people any more than the man influences the wild animal. The true force of corruption, Plato suggests, is the public at large, the movement of whose attitudes many people will find irresistible (492a ff.). The sophists here are represented as responding to, as opposed to shaping, wider social attitudes.[21] So although there are certainly passages in the shorter dialogues that present the sophists in a bad light, Plato's intention may not simply have been their humiliation.

I will conclude this section by making one final point. We have witnessed over the last 50 years or so a revival in the study of the virtues. This work has taken its inspiration from the writings of Plato and Aristotle. Philosophers consulting their works for insights into the nature of the virtues are likely to pay closer attention to the more reputable positions in their writings than to those obvious non-starters. One of the main reasons for the neglect of the views of the interlocutors, then, is because of their putative falsity. But the truth of the interlocutors' views may not have exhausted Plato's interest in them. These were, after all, popular views and they appealed to people of a certain intellectual taste. Euthyphro, for example, presents four different definitions of piety, but underpinning all of them is a commercial conception of the relationship between the gods and humankind. He thinks that god-fearingness is simply our end of the bargain: if we do right by them, we can effectively purchase their good favour. To what kind of person would such a conception appeal? Plato may have intended his readers to reflect on such matters before commencing the positive enterprise of trying to clarify the nature of the virtue.[22]

As I indicated above, the essays in Part Two will cover the relevant details of the principal interlocutors. In this section I have tried to suggest that we should be more open to their views than the line the professional literature in some cases encourages.

Plato

Plato appears in only one dialogue, the *Apology*, but he does not speak: his sole contribution is to bankroll Socrates' fine, which he proposes as an alternative to the capital sentence demanded by his prosecutors (38b). Unlike my earlier remarks about Socrates and his interlocutors, then, my comments here are not about a literary character, and as such are on even less of a sure footing. There's certainly no shortage of good stories about Plato: for instance that his real name was Aristocles, that his family descended from the god Apollo and that he was sold into, and bought out of, slavery following his first trip to Sicily. But there really was no genre of historical biography in his day and, by the time there was, the details of Plato's life were already interwoven with myth.

Rather than pick up on one or two points from our most recent efforts to separate fact from fiction, I will in this section make a couple of points that pertain more directly to our reading of these works. The first is that Plato's direct contact with Socrates, which strikes us as the most decisive aspect of his early life, occurred when Plato was quite young. Deborah Nails has recently suggested Plato was born as late as 424 and Diogenes Laertius claims that he first made Socrates' acquaintance when he was 20. Thus he would have known Socrates for a little over four years. Even if we accept Taylor's claim that Plato would have known Socrates since childhood, the Platonic dialogues are still the reflections of a young man looking back on what he remembered of an old man.

Now, it may be thought that very little hinges on this. Why does it matter that Plato was comparatively young when he had direct contact with Socrates? But some scholars think that Plato's account of Socrates' life is the only accurate one. This implies that Plato more or less fully comprehended the man and went on to reproduce some of his conversations in his writings. But we might equally imagine that Plato was fascinated and disturbed by Socrates and sought, through his writing, to clarify for himself the man and his thought. The dialogues would then represent Plato's ongoing effort to make sense of the man who in so short a space of time changed his life so much.

The second point concerns Plato's career. He was destined for a life in politics but, the story goes, he was so appalled by the conduct of The Thirty he turned his back on any such ambition and dedicated his life to science. Thus he founded the Academy in 383: a centre for education in Athens at which he conducted research and gave lectures. He then wrote a series of dialogues containing his discoveries. However, Pascal confounded this picture of Plato the academic: 'We always picture Plato and Aristotle wearing long academic gowns, but they were ordinary decent people … who enjoyed a laugh with their friends … if they wrote about politics it was as if to lay down rules for a madhouse'.[23] Furthermore, he never did turn his back on his political ambition, as his increasingly disastrous interventions in Sicily in the second quarter of the fourth century make plain. We do not know his motive in composing dialogues with a character called Socrates; whether they were for the purposes of teaching or whether they were for amusement. It is, then, frustratingly unclear how we are supposed to take these writings, but this should remind us that an author's interest and that of his readers need not necessarily coincide.[24]

Conclusion

In this chapter I have suggested that we are sometimes closer to the interlocutors of Plato's dialogues than we are to Socrates. A more exciting reading of Plato awaits those who imagine themselves the victims of Socratic *elenchus* as opposed to members of the Socratic chorus cheering the philosopher on. In the next chapter we will move away from these general matters and turn our attention to matters of philosophy.

CHAPTER TWO

How Socrates argues

Introduction

Plato's shorter dialogues represent Socrates as having a distinctive way of doing philosophy. He typically asks someone a *prima facie* straightforward question and then, having been given an answer, proceeds to ask several further questions.[1] The responses to these contradict the answer to the original question, which is then rejected. The repetition of this pattern across the dialogues is significant and many scholars have been tempted by the idea that Plato ascribes a single philosophical method to Socrates. The name for this method is the Socratic *elenchus* and commentators in the last century invested considerable energy in its examination.

There is a large and stimulating literature on Socratic methodology. This chapter does not pretend to advance our efforts to resolve the central and challenging questions that drive the debates in the field. The purpose is simply to prepare the ground for our reading of the dialogues: to notice and develop some of the principal characteristics of Socrates' approach.

There is, unhappily, no escaping the fairly technical character of the scholarship in this area. In working through the topic, however, we will start from the broadest possible perspective before zooming in on one or two matters of importance. Accordingly, we shall begin by considering the *elenchus* itself before moving to consider Socrates' 'What is F?' question, which typically initiates the explicitly philosophical discussion of the dialogues. It is then natural to consider Socrates' standard for what is to count as knowledge, his profession of ignorance, his distinctive mode of argument (the epagoge), and the problem of irony. Before we set off, however, I shall make one over-arching caveat: work in this area of Socratic studies is *ambitious*. It is the attempt to distil and codify a single methodological approach from a series of dramatic writings that may never have been intended to bear such patient scrutiny. Reflection and speculation informed by the shorter dialogues has, of course, borne great philosophical fruit: Whitehead's famous remark that Western Philosophy is little more than a series of footnotes to Plato reflects this truth. But equally some scholars hope to be able to pin down the philosophical method of this character, or characters if you resist the idea that Plato wrote with a unified portrait in mind. We should keep in mind the possibility that in this respect, at least, their ambition may exceed what the texts can be reasonably thought to deliver.

The Socratic *elenchus*

Reference to the idea of the *elenchus* is commonplace in the literature on Socrates and this may, to some extent, disguise its relatively recent origin. Although Gregory Vlastos traced its earliest use to George Grote in 1865, it was Richard Robinson who popularised the expression through his influential treatment of Plato in 1941.[2] I make this point because the currency of the term in the literature may give the misleading impression of consensus among commentators. But in recent years scholarship has been marked by scepticism. Indeed, two high profile scholars have even suggested that the Socratic *elenchus* is nothing more than an artefact of modern scholarship.[3] But even if this is correct, commentators face the question of what to say about the striking commonalities we find across a number of dialogues, and it is these features we will concentrate on in this section.

The standard picture of the *elenchus* looks like this. Socrates asks primary and secondary questions.[4] The primary question is often, but not always,[5] his 'What is F?'[6] question, where F designates the entities Socrates is interested in and about which his interlocutors profess to know. For example, 'Tell me, then, what do you say *piety* is?' (*Euthyphro* 5d). The secondary questions are more varied and raise issues more or less explicitly related to F. For example, 'Haven't we also said that the gods have quarrels with one another, Euthyphro, and disputes with one another, and that there is an enmity between them?' (ibid. 7b). Through asking these questions Socrates obtains a set of answers that are inconsistent with one another and then rejects the answer to the primary question. So, having been asked to define piety, Euthyphro states that prosecuting one's father for murder is pious. Socrates then obtains Euthyphro's agreement to the claim that many more things than that are pious. Therefore, prosecuting one's father for murder cannot be what makes an action pious (ibid. 5d–6e). This pattern repeats itself within the dialogue and culminates in *aporia*: a state of perplexity and failure.

It's when we try to clarify the standard picture, however, that we immediately run into interpretative difficulties. We notice, for instance, that the standard picture does not capture everything Socrates does in the dialogues. For, despite his avowed antipathy to anything other than exchanges comprising short question and answer, Socrates sometimes makes lengthy speeches.[7] We can, of course, set those passages aside because the presence of speeches doesn't imply that something like the standard picture is not Socrates' main, or even dominant, way of practising philosophy. Less easy to overlook, however, is a question about the rejection of answers to primary questions.

The Greek word '*elenchus*' means both testing or cross-examining and refuting.[8] For the last 30 years the modern debate has concentrated on the nature of the refutations Socrates secures. He has, recall, elicited a set of beliefs {P, Q, R} from his interlocutor, where P is the answer to his primary question. The set is inconsistent and so it follows that the conjunction {P & Q & R} is false. That implies the falsity of at least one of those beliefs; but which one? Socrates, as we have already noted, typically rejects P. The question that has dogged Socratic epistemology is on precisely what basis does he do so. After all, the inconsistency itself does not provide us with a reason for thinking this or that particular member of the set is false. This is what Vlastos dubbed the 'problem of the *elenchus*', and its solution or dissolution has been the focus of subsequent scholarly discussion.[9]

There are broadly two patterns of response to the problem of the *elenchus*. Some commentators, such as Vlastos himself, think that Socrates succeeds in demonstrating the falsity of individual propositions (e.g. ¬P). Other commentators, such as Hugh Benson, deny this and claim that the most Socrates can be said to have demonstrated is the falsity of the conjunction (i.e. ¬{P & Q & R}). For the sake of convenience we will use Benson's labels for these positions: he refers to Vlastos's position as constructivism and his own position as non-constructivism.[10] Although non-constructivists deny that Socrates demonstrates the falsity of any one proposition, their position is consistent with the possibility that Socrates succeeds in refuting his interlocutors' claims to possess knowledge (e.g. *Apology* 23a).

In terms of the history of Socratic scholarship, constructivism, in some form or other, has won more support. But as students of Plato we face the question ourselves: how can we determine which, if either, interpretation is correct? The most intuitive reaction is to take a look at what Socrates actually says: does he pronounce P demonstrably false or not? But unfortunately a review of the texts proves inconclusive on this point. There are some passages in which Socrates concludes that P is false (e.g. *Laches* 199e), but in others he explicitly states that the refutation of P is conditional and depends on the success of an argument. For example, 'Fineness, then, isn't good, nor is goodness fine. Don't you think that is ruled out *by our argument*?' (*Hippias Major* 297c).[11]

A more promising approach examines the epistemic status of answers to primary and secondary questions. If Socrates thinks that Q and R are better known than P, that would license his rejection of P.[12] Doyle, for example, claims that Socrates and his interlocutors have asserted Q and R, whereas P is only entertained as an hypothesis to be tested.[13] According to Vlastos, Socrates concludes '¬P' when he's only entitled to infer '(Q & R) → ¬P'. But the assertion of Q and R resolves this worry: Socrates isn't merely specifying what follows *if* Q and R are true, so far as he and his interlocutors are concerned they actually *are* true. This response to the problem of the *elenchus* assumes that Socrates and his interlocutors think of themselves as testing hypotheses. But that doesn't ring true when we examine the texts. Take Meno, for example, who is asked to define virtue. He prefaces his answer with the claim that 'there is no difficulty about it' (71e). So far as he's concerned, he knows the answer and is not putting forward a reasonable suggestion to be tested (see also *Laches* 190e and *Hippias Major* 286e).

Instead of reviewing direct responses to Vlastos's problem, which runs the risk of seeing the scholarly debate spiral off into obscurity, we will keep our feet on the ground and consider the goal of the *elenchus*. If it is intended to deliver constructive results, that will motivate the search for indications in the text that justify Socrates' inference of '¬P'.

The plausibility of constructivism derives from the assumption that Socrates is conducting a genuine inquiry into the nature of F. If that's what he's up to, then he must be trying to establish the truth about F. But if truth is his goal, the apparent abandonment of accounts of F on the strength of mere inconsistency is surprising. A person responsibly inquiring into the nature of F would ensure that the answers to secondary questions were true before moving to reject the answer to the primary question. Here lies the original motivation for constructivism: Socrates simply must have reason to think the answers to the secondary questions are true. But this entire line of thought is premised on the assumption that Socrates is conducting a genuine inquiry and we might wonder whether we're entitled to make such an assumption.

Now, Socrates does sometimes state that he is conducting an inquiry (e.g. *Charmides* 165b and *Meno* 80d). But in his most explicit comments about his philosophical activity he calls such claims into question. In the *Apology* Socrates makes two comments that repay reflection. First, he claims he sets out to refute people only *after* he has decided they did not know what they were talking about (23b). This undermines the image of Socrates working with colleagues to try to identify F. Second, Socrates claims that his work consists in the exhortation of his fellow citizens to care more for their souls than their bank balances (29d). This suggests Socrates has a specific ethical lesson to teach. Superficially, these look like divergent aims but they would appear to be complementary: he grounds his exhortation in the refutation of his interlocutors' existing beliefs about how to live.[14] But if exhortation is his primary aim, it wouldn't even be necessary to refute the proposed definition of F: it would only be necessary that the interlocutor *believed* it refuted.

Importantly, the account of Socrates' goal contained in the *Apology* chimes with the other dialogues. First, Socrates is very keen to stress the interlocutors' claims to know what F is. Euthyphro, he maintains, would never have undertaken so controversial and grave a course of action unless he actually *knew* it was the right thing to do (*Euthyphro* 4a). Second, Socrates sometimes emphasises that his interlocutors should only answer with what they really believe in response to secondary questions (e.g. *Laches* 193c; *Gorgias* 474a–b; and *Protagoras* 331c).[15] But why, if Socrates is concerned with the truth or falsity of the definition of F, should he be so concerned about what his interlocutor claims to know or believe? The interlocutor's definition will be true or false, but, it's natural to think, its truth or falsity will not be determined by the interlocutor's mere possession of other beliefs that entail or contradict it. If, on the other hand, Socrates is trying to refute his interlocutor's claim to possess knowledge, then an examination of what he claims to know and believe is to the point because an *elenchus* reveals his commitment to P and ¬P.

There is, of course, much more to be said. First, why should we privilege the evidence of the *Apology* in this way? In any case, Carpenter and Polansky, for example, dispute the assumption that there is a single form of the *elenchus*.[16] If that's true, the dialogues exhibit at most variations on a theme as opposed to the application of a single pattern of argument. Second, the significance of Socrates' demand that his interlocutors say only what they believe is controversial. Wolfsdorf, for example, claims that Socrates is seeking confirmation for what he calls F-conditions (conditions that determine the identity of F) because he, Socrates, professes not to know the F-conditions for F.[17] The point is that Socrates is looking for evidence for F-conditions and the endorsement of others gives him a reason to suppose that these are the conditions an account of F must meet.

But both these lines of criticism return us to our original question about the goal of the *elenchus*. It seems to me reasonably clear that Socrates is not straightforwardly undertaking philosophical research. He is not a Professor of Philosophy. If he was, why does he pick these particular men as colleagues in the enterprise? Why is there not a dialogue representing Socrates in conversation with someone his equal, such as Plato himself? These questions, of course, invite further speculation and we must bring the discussion to a close.

In sum, Socrates was clearly interested in the nature of virtue. As he remarks in the *Laches*, he had cultivated a fascination for the topic since he was a boy (186c). But Plato equally represents him as conspicuously interested in the claims of people to know about virtue. It is specifically these claims that he seeks to examine and he resists the temptation to use their suggestions as springboards to further his own inquiry. Thus I think it is more profitable to think of the *elenchus* in the first instance as testing his interlocutors' boastful claims to know about matters of the greatest consequence.

The 'What is F?' question

We have already referred in passing to the 'What is F?' question in the previous section. Patently, the formulation 'What is F?' is an abstraction and nowhere in the shorter dialogues does Socrates consider the question in such terms. Specific examples include: 'What do you say piety and impiety are? (*Euthyphro* 9c); 'Try to put into words what bravery is' (*Laches* 190e); and 'Tell me ... what you say temperance is in your opinion' (*Charmides* 159a). The 'What is F?' question appears in eight of the 14 shorter dialogues and in each case indicates the principal matter of philosophical interest.[18] In this section we will consider what assumptions Socrates makes in asking 'What is F?' and what conditions he places on satisfactory responses. But we'll begin, though, by considering why he places such emphasis on this question.

Socrates frequently contends that we have to answer the question 'What is F?' before we can go on and determine the solution to some other issue.[19] For example, Socrates feels he can't make a judgement about the value of hoplomachy – a form of military training – until he knows what bravery is (*Laches*), nor can he state with confidence whether virtue can be taught until he knows what virtue is (*Meno*). The necessity of knowing F in order to know at least some things about F is referred to politely as the 'priority of definitional knowledge' and impolitely as 'the Socratic Fallacy'.[20]

As far as Socrates is concerned, then, arriving at adequate responses to 'What is F?' is of decisive importance for the determination of a range of issues in human life. We will begin our consideration of this question by examining the assumptions Socrates makes in posing it at all. In the first instance, he assumes the question can be answered in words.[21] The obviousness of this assumption conceals its potential controversy: philosophers, after all, take very seriously the question about the extent to which languages can accurately represent how things are.[22] However, Socrates seems to think that the existence of F implies the possibility of our describing it in words. He tells Charmides, for example, that if he is temperate, he will be able to say what it is (*Charmides* 158e; cf. *Laches* 190c). But if we briefly step outside the Platonic corpus, we find Xenophon suggesting that this is not the only possibility: Socrates tells the sophist Hippias that his 'deeds are better evidence [of his knowledge of justice] than words' (*Memorabilia* 4.4.10–11).

Second, Socrates sometimes emphasises, and seeks his interlocutors' agreement, that there is such a thing as F (e.g. *Hippias Major* 287c and *Protagoras* 330d). Now, plainly, if there is no such thing as F, there is no prospect of our providing an account of it. But some scholars have thought this assumption is more ontologically loaded than that. Robinson, for example, thinks Socrates is committed to a form of realism, which he thinks implies that F is in some sense mind-independent.[23] It is, however, unclear whether the texts sustain the point: in his translation of the *Hippias Major*, Waterfield notes that 'Socrates is exploiting the linguistic form of the sentence which makes it *seem* that justice etc. are external to their possessors'.[24] This suggests that the original Greek falls short of a full-blooded assertion of mind-independence.

Now, conventionally, scholars have treated the 'What is F?' question as an invitation for interlocutors to provide a definition of F. In the literature this claim is typically followed by the qualification that Socrates is *not* seeking a dictionary definition of F. The consensus on this point is striking, but we may wonder why a dictionary definition would be inadequate. The point is that a dictionary definition specifies something about the way we use a word. But with respect to usage, Socrates and his interlocutors are typically in agreement. Laches, for example, says that a man who remains at his post under fire from the enemy is brave, and Socrates concurs (*Laches* 190e–191a). They're both, then, reasonably competent users of the term 'brave'. The point commentators have in mind when they rule out dictionary definitions is simply that we should not mistake this sort of competency for knowledge of what F really is. We can get a vivid sense of this when we think about the case of pleasure. We're all competent with the use of the term, but even the great Aristotle was reduced to 'sheer babble' when he tried to state what it really is.[25]

The possession of a dictionary definition, then, will not confer knowledge of the nature of F. What Socrates seeks is a real, as opposed to a nominal, definition.[26] A real definition of F will be a description of the essence of F. But how do we know whether a given description specifies the essence of F? There are two principal conditions an adequate definition must meet: the substitutivity and the explanatory conditions.[27] There are other conditions, but clarity with respect to these two will be sufficient for us now.

The substitutivity condition stipulates that G is an adequate definition of F, if we can substitute G for F in propositions about F *salva veritate*. Consider Laches's first attempt to define bravery: a man is brave if he remains at his post while under fire from the enemy (ibid.). If 'remaining at his post while under fire from the enemy' were an adequate definition of 'bravery', then we would be able to substitute one for the other in sentences about bravery without affecting their truth-value. But according to Socrates this is not what we find. It could be true that someone was brave and yet false that he remained at his post. How so? Because, says Socrates, that person could be a Scythian who is brave but fights in retreat and does *not* remain at his post (191b).

Socrates frequently tests interlocutors' definitions by examining whether they meet the substitutivity condition. But we may doubt whether meeting that condition is sufficient for the identification of F. To use a reasonably familiar example, the terms 'cordate' and 'renate' are co-extensive and meet the substitutivity condition. If the statement 'This animal is a cordate' is true, then the statement 'This animal is a renate' will be true too. But these terms mean different things: 'cordate' refers to things with hearts and 'renate' to things with kidneys. Philosophers resolve the problem here by pointing out that 'cordate' and 'renate' are only contingently, and not necessarily, co-extensive: we can imagine a possible world in which something is a renate but not a cordate. So it looks like necessary co-extensivity implies identity, but some philosophers dispute this: it would appear that there are cases of necessarily co-extensive terms that vary in meaning.[28] However, whether or not such examples can be made out, this is not a problem for Socrates because G must also meet his explanatory condition, which rules out the possibility of mere compresence.

The explanatory condition itself formally states that G is an adequate definition of F if G explains why all F-things are F.

Examples of Socrates stating this condition include: 'I asked you for that special feature [eidos] *through which* all pious things are pious' (*Euthyphro* 6d–e); and '... the fine itself, the form, which *when present makes* everything else as well attractive and appear fine ...' (*Hippias Major* 289d). The explanatory condition rule guarantees that the presence of G is responsible for the F-ness of this or that particular thing.

It is instructive to look at an example of a definition from the *Meno* that fails to meet the explanatory condition. Meno asks Socrates to define shape. 'It is', he replies, 'the only thing that always accompanies colour' (Meno 75b). Now this meets the substitutivity condition, but not the explanatory condition because 'being the only thing that always accompanies colour' does not explain what makes shaped things shaped.[29] Contrast this with Socrates' definition of clay as 'earth mixed with liquid' (*Theatetus* 147c). In this case, it is because something is earth mixed with liquid that it is clay and so this definition meets the explanatory condition.[30]

So, in reply to his 'What is F?' question Socrates anticipates a description of F that meets both the substitutivity and explanatory conditions. But we should bear in mind just how controversial Socrates' programme is by modern philosophical tastes. Wittgenstein, for example, contested the presumption that there would be a single set of criteria for the application of a term. Instead, there may be a family resemblance: a cluster of characteristics no one of which is necessary for the use of the term.[31] Take games: if we were to suppose that a game must have a winner, Wittgenstein points to a child bouncing a ball against a wall and catching it. This is a game but there is no winner. Socrates' question, then, may be predicated on what is by modern standards a very controversial assumption.

We will frequently refer to Socrates' 'What is F?' question and the conditions for an adequate answer in the discussions of the individual dialogues in Part Two. The reflections in this section will be especially salient to the appraisal of the *Meno*, in which Socrates appears to state a preference for something other than a real definition (*Meno* 76e).

Knowledge and ignorance

Socrates famously didn't say 'I only know that I know nothing'. The passage from the *Apology* actually reads: 'I am only too conscious that I have no claim to wisdom, great or small' (21b). He expresses what is superficially the same point in several other dialogues.[32] These statements collectively foster the impression that Socrates' avowed ignorance is pretty much global. But this impression sits uneasily, to say the least, with his remarks elsewhere. In the *Euthydemus*, for example, he claims he knows lots of things, albeit unimportant things (293b). More significant claims to possess knowledge emerge in the *Apology* (29b), in which Socrates claims to know it's wrong to disobey a superior, and in the *Meno* (98b), in which Socrates clams to know the distinction between knowledge and true belief.

Scholars have attempted to resolve the apparent inconsistency between these texts in various ways. Norman Gulley, for example, denies the sincerity of Socrates' disavowal of knowledge: it is, he thinks, a rhetorical device that facilitates participation from others by flattering their self-esteem.[33] Other commentators take Socrates at his word and try to explain the apparent inconsistency away. Vlastos, for example, argues that Socrates has two conceptions of knowledge, strong and weak; Socrates can truthfully deny he has knowledge in the strong sense while professing to have knowledge in the weak sense.[34]

Quite what to make of Socrates' admission of ignorance is clearly one of the enduring puzzles about him. I raise the matter in this chapter because a person who claims he knows some things but not others is operating with a standard for what counts as knowledge. Now, Vlastos points out that the Socrates of the early dialogues was exclusively a moral philosopher and not an epistemologist.[35] Putting aside the issue of whether we can intelligibly discriminate early and middle dialogues, Vlastos's claim seems true of the Socrates of a number of shorter dialogues in the following sense. He does not submit to elenctic scrutiny claims about what it is for a person to know something about the world. He doesn't, for example, invite Euthyphro to state what he thinks knowledge is and then proceed to appraise his answer. But it doesn't follow that Socrates is not applying more or less consistently some standard of knowledge. The question for commentators is precisely what that standard might be.

The problem, though, is that the texts are silent on the matter. Socrates' professions of ignorance, for example, are simply asserted: he tells Meno he doesn't know what virtue is and that he hasn't met anyone who does know either (71b–d). He doesn't, however, explain how he arrived at this judgement, which would cast some light on his standard of knowledge. Commentators working in this area are obliged to look elsewhere to piece together whatever conception of knowledge Socrates has.

When Socrates claims in the conclusions to aporetic dialogues that the participants in the conversation have failed to identify F, it is on the basis of the repeated application of the *elenchus* (e.g. *Euthyphro* 15c and *Laches* 199e). This naturally suggests that Socrates thinks a person possesses knowledge about virtue if his views about virtue survive elenctic scrutiny.[36] That is, the consistency of your answer to Socrates' 'What is F?' question with your other beliefs is a necessary condition for your claim to possess knowledge. We should note, first of all, that surviving elenctic scrutiny should not be thought of as comprising a single episode of interrogation: in the *Crito,* Socrates reappraises elenctically robust views, which suggests the process is ongoing (46b-c).[37] But while we might concede that surviving the *elenchus* is necessary for knowledge we may wonder whether it's sufficient. That is to say that a person may fairly claim to know what has survived repeated applications of the *elenchus*.

So far as Socrates is concerned, we cannot answer this question. None of the proposed definitions in the shorter dialogues meets the test and we have no instances of Socrates' next move. Some commentators have argued that a person could claim to have greater confidence in a definition that repeatedly resisted elenctic refutation, but the question here is whether greater confidence constitutes knowledge.[38] The *Crito* appears to be a case in point: Socrates concludes that he should not flee because it would be unjust (54d). But the reader may feel anyway that we're getting ahead of ourselves. We might wonder, though, whether Socrates would be right to think elenctic robustness is necessary for knowledge in the first place.

The worry is that Socrates' standard of knowledge is too high. If we claim that surviving repeated elenctic examination is a necessary condition of knowing F, then it seems the interlocutors do not know F at all. But we typically think that we know quite a lot about the world and so Socrates' standard of knowledge is not the standard we use in everyday life. It's worth comparing matters here with Descartes who is also sometimes thought to have set the bar for knowledge impossibly high by appearing to demand certainty for the retention of a belief. Descartes anticipates this complaint in the *Discourse on Method*:

> For a long time I had remarked that it is sometimes requisite in common life to follow opinions one knows to be most uncertain, exactly as though they were indisputable ... But because in this case I wished to give myself entirely to the search after Truth, I thought it was necessary for me to take an apparently opposite course and to reject as false everything as to which I could imagine the least ground of doubt.[39]

In this passage Descartes qualifies the application of the Method of Doubt: it is restricted to a pure search for truth and is not the criterion of knowledge we use in ordinary life. This is because Descartes is concerned with what, if anything, we can *really* know. But matters are quite the other way around with Socrates: he assumes that our practical decisions must be based on knowledge of F (e.g. *Laches* and *Crito*). Unlike Descartes, Socrates thinks that knowledge in his sense lies at the core of everyday life. This throws into question a considerable number of our decisions. But that is Socrates' point: practical decisions of the utmost gravity are all too often based on the thinnest grounds. He tells Crito, for example, that the general public are frivolous and think nothing over matters of life and death (48c). The reader is left with the question of how to proceed in daily life in the absence of elenctically robust beliefs.

But even if we were to argue that Socrates is not operating with our everyday conception of knowledge in mind, there remains the question whether our conception is fit for purpose. Perhaps we should loosen our sense of self-righteousness in light of the awareness we reach through following Socrates' argument that we do not possess knowledge in the stronger sense he pursued.

As this brief survey has revealed, we only arrive at something like Socrates' conception of knowledge through inferences from his conduct in the dialogues. This outline, then, is speculative. Readers interested in pursuing the matter further should consult Benson (2006) and Wolfsdorf (2003), whose close and patient scholarship reveal how far the texts may take us in this area.

Epagoge

'You simply never stop talking of cobblers and fullers and doctors; as if our argument were concerned with them.' So Callicles chides Socrates for referring to artisans in a discussion ostensibly about natural right (*Gorgias* 490e–491a). His remark is likely to resonate with many readers of Plato's dialogues who notice the frequency with which Socrates refers to expertise of all kinds in his secondary questions. Consider the following passage selected at random. Laches's second definition of bravery is wise endurance. Socrates wonders whether it is actually the absence of specialist expertise that renders action brave. In the course of making this point he refers to horsemanship, slinging, archery and the practice of diving in wells (*Laches* 193b–c). His choice of examples is striking and one could make a profitable study of precisely why Socrates reaches for this or that particular expertise in a given instance. But with respect to our present purpose, Socrates' manner of philosophising, we will consider the nature of the arguments in which they appear.

Aristotle states in a much quoted passage that two things could be ascribed to Socrates: epagogic arguments and universal definitions (*Metaphysics* 1078b 27–8). Most English editions translate 'epagoge' as 'induction' and so it seems that we have it on good authority that Socrates' arguments about cobblers and farmers are inductive generalisations to probabilistic conclusions. So, to continue the example above, Socrates infers from these four cases, in which the absence rather than the presence of specialist expertise renders actions brave, that bravery is (probably) a form of ignorance. However, Robinson claims he is hard pressed to point to a single passage in the corpus of an inductive generalisation.[40]

But induction is only one of three conceptions of epagoge Robinson identifies. The others are the intuition of a universal and deduction from a complete enumeration of cases.[41] I take the reader to be familiar with deductive forms of argument and so will not comment on them here. The intuition of a universal, on the other hand, is more obscure and readers are unlikely to have encountered it before. The rest of this section will focus on that form of epagoge.

Vlastos distinguishes the intuition of a universal from an inductive generalisation in terms of the relationship between the premises and the conclusion. The premises of an inductive generalisation render the conclusion probable: they document evidence of a limited number of cases from which a universal conclusion is inferred. Such arguments are vulnerable to refutation by the production of counter-examples: thus the Australian black swan refutes the conclusion that all swans are white. But matters are not like that with the intuition of a universal: the premises of that form of argument do not provide empirical support for the conclusion; they communicate the *meaning of the conclusion*.[42]

Vlastos gives the following example from the *Ion* (540bff.):

(i) The steersman knows best what to say to the captain of the ship's crew in a storm

(ii) The doctor knows best what to say to those who tend the ailing

(iii) The cowherd knows best what to say to those who tend angry cattle

(iv) The expert in wool knows best what to say to women working with wool

(v) The military expert knows best what the general should say to the troops

So,

(vi) The expert of a craft knows best about matters that fall within its subject matter

If this was an inductive generalisation, the conclusion (vi) would be weakened by the deletion of a premise. But the strength of (vi), Vlastos points out, is written into the meaning of the expression 'expert of a craft': someone who does not possess superior knowledge of the subject matter is, by that very fact, not an expert of that craft. We would refrain from calling a person 'expert' if he did not possess superior knowledge of a given subject matter. The truth of this does not depend on the premises in the way the conclusion of an inductive inference does, and so we could delete premise (v), say, without weakening (vi) at all. Strictly speaking, then, the intuition of a universal does not constitute an inference from premises to conclusion at all.

The intuition of a universal is, to my mind, an intriguing and puzzling form of epagoge. In the case that Vlastos cites from the *Ion*, the conclusion (vi) appears to be a tautology. But if all the conclusions of this form of epagoge are tautologies, it appears to render mysterious the issue this communicative function is designed to overcome. Mark McPherran, however, points out that the premises are intended to obtain the interlocutor's assent through explanation.[43] He further notices, contrary to Robinson's assertion, that there are instances of inductive generalisation (e.g. *Euthyphro* 7a–8a).[44] The point to take away, then, is that there are various forms of epagoge and that a complete appraisal of the arguments of the shorter dialogues will require our sensitivity to the nuances of particular passages.

Socratic and Platonic irony

Socrates is famous for irony; Plato is not. But the irony of both the character and the author cast a shadow over the interpretation of the dialogues and present us with a puzzle. We cannot hope in this section to resolve the enduring questions about Socratic irony, but we can hope to distinguish its usage and note implications for those of us reading the dialogues carefully.

Vlastos famously argued that Socrates was responsible for a change in the use of the Greek word '*eiron*'.[45] This originally denoted a dissembler, an instructive sense of which we can find in Theophrastus:

> The dissembler is the sort who goes up to his enemies and is willing to chat with them. He praises to their faces those whom he has attacked in secret and commiserates with people he is suing if they lose their case ... He admits to nothing that he is actually doing but says he is thinking it over ... If he has heard something he pretends he hasn't and says he hasn't seen something he has ... He is apt to employ phrases like this: 'I don't believe it', 'I don't think so', 'I'm astonished' and 'You're telling me he's become a different person'.[46]

The core of dissemblance, then, is *deception*. When a dissembler denies having heard something, he intends an audience to take him at his word. Dissemblance succeeds just when an auditor comes to possess a false belief. But irony for us is not like that. For example, this morning I was wrestling with a bag of ground coffee which, when it finally gave way, showered both me and the kitchen floor in 250g of coffee. 'That's a good start to the day,' I said to my wife. She smiled as I went fetch the dustpan. The irony of my remark succeeded: my wife understood that I didn't mean what I said. She did not come to possess the false belief that I thought the day had started well. Deception, then, which is the core of dissemblance, plays no part in our conception of irony.

Although the precise character of Socratic irony is controversial,[47] I will plough ahead on the basis that Socrates is not out to straightforwardly deceive his interlocutors. Given the difference between the success conditions of irony and dissemblance, then, it is remarkable how infrequently Socrates' irony succeeds on its apparent targets. Many of his interlocutors are insensitive to its application and continue to take the conversation at face value. Take, for example, Ion, the successful rhapsode. He insists that his expertise in discoursing upon Homer extends to no other poets (*Ion* 531a). Socrates explores his claim and provides him with an argument that demonstrates his expertise with *all* the poets. Ion accepts the argument but denies the conclusion and thereby misses Socrates' real point that Ion is no expert at all. The failure of the irony reveals itself most plainly when Ion is flattered into acknowledging that he is among the greatest of military leaders (ibid. 541b). There are, of course, passages in which interlocutors recognise that something is afoot (e.g. *Gorgias* 489e; *Symposium* 216e; *Republic* 337a). But equally there are entire dialogues in which interlocutors miss it altogether (e.g. *Euthyphro* and *Hippias Major*).

As readers, though, we seldom miss the ironies Socrates practises upon his interlocutors. We laugh at Ion's failure to realise Socrates wasn't suggesting for one moment that he was a superior military general and at Hippias' apparent innocence regarding the identity of Socrates' 'friend'. But it is in precisely these respects that we may be beguiled into missing the ironies Plato practises upon his readers.[48] In the previous chapter, we noted that we are less like Socrates and more like his interlocutors than we'd care to admit.

Our ready arrival at such a belief is, for Nehamas, a success of Plato's dark irony. We will consider one instance of this before reflecting on the implications for our reading of the dialogues.

In the *Hippias Minor* Hippias accuses Socrates of arguing unfairly (369bff.). Socrates denies this: he wouldn't waste his time speaking to Hippias unless he genuinely thought he could learn something from him. The reader knows that Socrates is not going to learn anything about the ostensible topic of conversation. But even if that's true, it doesn't follow that Socrates believes there is nothing whatsoever to learn from him. Hippias, for example, is an academic and a sophist. When practising sophistry he teaches the eristic, the art of victory of speech (see *Hippias Major*). The success of eristic, like the success of advertising, lies in an understanding of certain common patterns of thinking. If, for example, I persuade you that there are, counterfactually, only two options and that one of them is conspicuously less palatable than the other, I might succeed in winning your assent to that alternative. In this case, my victory is secured once I have persuaded you of the limited number of options: you unfold the result of your own accord. Sophists, then, provide a window on the typical movements of the human soul and this illuminates the tendency among human beings to attach themselves to falsehoods.[49]

Nehamas' point is that Plato's irony flatters our sense of our own intelligence and thus creates in us the impoverished stance of the interlocutors who believe they know more than they do. This has clear implications for the reader. One reaction is to determine not to be a dupe: to examine the text with such vigilance that one does not succumb to Plato's irony. That may well be possible, but also looks like one more case of misplaced confidence. If we think of the dialogues primarily as exhibitions of a process, the experience of being 'taken in' is a constituent of appreciating Plato's point. We should, therefore, bring our awareness of Plato's irony to those assessments we make in the reading of the dialogues.

Conclusion

The scholarship considered in this chapter constitutes a discrete, and firmly established, area of study. I would like to remind the reader at this point that the purpose here was, in the first instance, to raise awareness of the issues surrounding Socrates' approach to philosophy with a view to deepening our appreciation of it. I have suggested that Socrates is primarily concerned to examine his interlocutors' claims to possess knowledge through the evaluation of their responses to his primary questions. Where his primary question is his 'What is F?' question, there are (at least) two conditions adequate answers must meet: the substitutivity and explanatory conditions. Socrates sometimes obtains assent to answers to secondary questions through the use of epagoge, which is used inductively and as a means of persuasion through explanation. Finally, the matter of Socrates' irony should not be reduced to straightforward deception: frequently his remarks are designed to do more than simply conceal his true position.

PART TWO

CHAPTER THREE

Apology

Introduction

The *Apology* comprises Socrates' defence speeches and his cross-examination of the principal prosecutor, Meletus. The text is universally acknowledged to be fundamentally important to the reading of Plato. It is, for example, thought to hold the key to the Socratic Problem.[1] If the *Apology* is an accurate account of what Socrates said in court, then it constitutes a standard against which we can test the other dialogues and establish a body of thought that is genuinely Socratic.[2]

But the historical interest of the *Apology* is not confined to the solution it promises to this enduring scholarly issue. The trial and execution of Socrates are themselves of the greatest significance. Indeed, one recent biographer has stated that 'the only death of comparable importance to our history is that of Jesus'.[3] If that's true, we are naturally going to take a special interest in the extant accounts of the trial to illuminate the meaning of these events. Plato's account, in particular, commands our attention because he states he was present at the trial (34a). Xenophon's *Apology*, the only other surviving account, is stated to be merely a report of what Hermogenes told him about the trial.[4]

There's no denying the intriguing nature of these discussions, but we are students of philosophy and not history. The question for us is quite what, if any, philosophical significance the *Apology* possesses. In his speeches Socrates does make reference to some of the philosophical theses scholars conventionally ascribe to him, such as the impossibility of voluntary wrongdoing (25e ff.). But what we find in the text is the application of these views and not an inquiry into their truth. The theme that does emerge, however, is the value, and in particular the justice, of philosophy itself. We are used, nowadays, to think of justice in connection with issues of equality, fair treatment and the acknowledgement of rights. But when I say here that Socrates defends the philosophical enterprise against allegations that it is unjust, I mean by 'justice' the most general term evaluating the right and proper conduct towards, and involving, others.

The dramatic date of the *Apology* is attested by all the sources: the spring of 399. The date of its composition, however, is disputed. Stylometric analysis, controversial in any case, has failed to place the *Apology* in the order of Plato's compositions with any precision. Modern estimates suggest it was written during the decade following Socrates' execution. But the idea that Plato wrote it soon after the trial, when the facts were still fresh in his mind, remains speculative and has not been adequately corroborated.[5]

The drama

As authors of courtroom dramas know to their profit, few events are as charged and compelling as the scene of a person fighting for his life. The action of the *Apology* begins, as Plato's title suggests, after Socrates' prosecutors have already made their case. We do not know what they have said and there are only few inferences we can make from the text itself (17a–b; 29c; 31d; 34a).[6] We cannot, then, appraise whether Socrates successfully answers the arguments presented by the prosecution. But this is beside the point. The defence speech Plato has Socrates deliver is itself intended to be a constituent of his ongoing divine mission: his purpose, as we shall see, is clearly not limited to guaranteeing his acquittal.

The charges against Socrates are well known: impiety and corruption. Precisely why he was thus charged, and why specifically in 399, has been a fruitful source of speculation among commentators. In the *Apology* Socrates initially states that Meletus was encouraged to draw up his indictment because of the widespread hostility towards him among the general public (19a–b). But this can't be the whole story: Socrates acknowledges that he already had an established reputation for sophistry in 423 when Aristophanes wrote *The Clouds* (18d; 19c). Other high profile intellectuals, such as Anaxagoras and Protagoras, were targeted for prosecution around that time.[7] Socrates, then, could have been brought to trial some 20 years earlier. Plato, in fact, represents him as conscious of the possibility of a prosecution in the years leading up to 399. The *Gorgias* is set around 405 and includes a passage in which Socrates refers explicitly to a trial: he will be like 'a doctor brought before a tribunal of children at the suit of a confectioner' (521c–e).

Socrates later suggests an underlying vengeful motive. His accusers represent three specific offended parties: the politicians, the poets and the artisans (20eff.). In the course of testing their respective claims to knowledge, Socrates succeeded in earning the enmity of them all. The charges are, then, nothing more than a pretext for revenge (23e–24a). Plato elsewhere lends some substance to this suggestion: he represents Socrates falling out with Anytus, one of his accusers, by praising the sophists he despises (*Meno* 91c). The discussion ends on a conspicuously menacing note: 'You seem to me, Socrates, to be too ready to run people down. My advice to you is to be careful. I dare say that in all cities it is easier to do a man harm than good and it is certainly so here' (ibid. 94e–95a).

But neither the general public hostility nor the specific rancour of the politicians, poets and artisans explains why Socrates was prosecuted in 399. One influential view, going back to Polycrates, is that the charges concealed a political motive. After the defeat of Athens in 404, a group of 30 pro-Spartan officials were appointed to govern the city. These men unleashed a reign of terror across the city: people were 'disappeared' in the middle of the night and thousands were killed in a festival of violence. This ultimately gave rise to a civil war, the outcome of which was the restoration of democracy in 403. We find Aeschines claiming in 345 that the Athenians killed Socrates for having educated Critias, the most notoriously violent member of The Thirty.[8]

Although scholars have been tempted by the idea that a political subtext explains the prosecution, the *Apology* makes no explicit references to Socrates' role in recent events. Nevertheless the trial was clearly political in character. Religion and politics are not distinct spheres of life and an accusation of impiety carried strong overtones of injustice. Socrates may have long been regarded as eccentric and annoying, but the reign of The Thirty would have exposed the danger he represented. The discussion with Meno takes place in 403, after the restoration. Anytus witnesses Socrates talking to his guest, Meno, an ambitious young man who would go on to betray Athens in 401. His parting words to Meno are that virtue is not knowledge but divine inspiration. Thus Anytus ostensibly sees Socrates packing off a dangerous young man, having apparently advised him he has nothing to learn about virtue and should simply 'follow his heart'. To outsiders, this would appear to be the continuation of Socrates' corrosive influence: a once merely eccentric teacher had finally turned political subversive.[9] And under cross-examination, Meletus confirms that it is because of what he has been teaching that he finds himself in court.

The justice of philosophy

John Stuart Mill[10] illustrated his petition for freedom of speech with reference to the trial of Socrates: that 'memorable collision' between the philosopher, the authorities and public opinion.[11] Mill thought that 'there ought to exist the fullest liberty of professing and discussing, as a matter of ethical conviction, any doctrine, however immoral it may be considered'.[12] We know Socrates was officially condemned for the profession of controversial doctrines, specifically his denial of the gods recognised by the state. So the core issue for Mill was the right to express ideas that conflicted with the prevailing orthodoxy in Athens. This reading of the *Apology* remains popular today[13] and garners some support from Socrates' defiant insistence that he will continue philosophising come what may (29d).

It's striking, then, that nowhere in Plato's *Apology* does Socrates claim he has an unrestricted right to verbal and non-verbal expression.[14] Instead he argues that philosophy is the best thing a person can do (38a) and that his life's work is the *greatest* gift the god has bestowed upon Athens (30a). Socrates seems to think philosophy itself is in the dock and sets himself up as its defence attorney. The question is whether philosophy stands in need of a defence.

The idea that philosophy might be dangerous does not resonate as it once did. But we should remember that there have been notable occasions in our history when philosophers have been eyed with suspicion. Hobbes, for example, was cited in the House of Commons in 1666 as a suspected cause of the plague. Bishops at the time murmured there wouldn't be any harm in burning him as a heretic.[15] More recently the City College of New York stripped Bertrand Russell of his professorship in 1940 for depravity and Yale dismissed Charles Stevenson in 1945 for the promotion of immorality.

These cases might give us pause to wonder whether philosophy really is as politically innocuous an exercise as it is sometimes thought to be. A useful starting point is the constitution of the state itself. The possibility of the state is dependent upon a commitment to shared ideas and values among its members. These ideas and values are handed down from one generation to the next as something like articles of faith. We can make out the significance of this through the consideration of the familiar institution of money. The continuation of this institution depends upon our all treating these bits of paper and metal as repositories of a power to facilitate action. If people lose their faith in money, the institution collapses: the presentation of a note or a coin would no longer engender activity as it once did.[16] The state, then, is vulnerable to dissolution should its members resign their commitment to its ideas and values.

The most conspicuous point of conflict between philosophy and the state would appear to be philosophical pronouncements that are at odds with its norms or laws. Peter Singer, for example, advocates euthanasia in some circumstances, but this conflicts with the law in the USA that proscribes euthanasia. However, the threat posed by philosophy is not simply the assertion of contradictory judgements: Singer's appointment to Princeton actually galvanised opposition to euthanasia among some groups. The real issue is that philosophy exploits and fosters an expanded intellectual space of possibilities. Philosophy teachers invite students to consider a range of issues, such as the existence of a mind-independent world or the possibility of an amoralist (a person who does not recognise the obligatory character of moral norms). The sovereignty, the ultimate authority, of the state is likewise situated in this wider intellectual context. Philosophers can, for example, ask whether the exercise of coercive power against citizens is, in any circumstances, legitimate.

The state, just like everything else, is simply one more thing that may be appraised in the intellectual space philosophy creates.

The inconclusive nature of philosophical discussions arguably makes matters worse because it suggests that much of the world we inherit is a sham. Young people are told that there are such things as right and wrong, but philosophical discussion is characteristically inconclusive. Regular exposure to such discussion has the potential to undermine citizens' commitment to the state's values.[17] A philosophy lecturer once whispered to me that he felt responsible for the development of quasi-nihilistic graduates who set foot on the world stage confident in their belief that they've seen behind the veil of ignorance no-one else even knows is there.

But as students of philosophy we are likely to contest this line of thought. In the first place, philosophical reflection is to some extent inevitable. We are curious creatures, we owe our development to our curiosity, and with leisure we cannot help but reflect on the nature of our world. After all, 'all men by nature desire to know', even if they do not carry their thoughts very much further.[18] In the second place, and more importantly, philosophy constitutes a check on blind dogma. History is littered with instances of people acting on beliefs we now think are deplorable, such as the murder of women believed to be witches. At the time of writing there is widespread public discussion of gay marriage. Orthodoxy proclaims marriage to be an institution between one man and one woman. But the effect of orthodoxy is the denigration of gay relationships. Future generations may come to regard that orthodoxy as outdated and deplorable. But the possibility of that depends on careful discussion in a philosophical context.

Points like these are persuasive, and persuade me, but they do not answer the charge that philosophy poses a threat. Philosophy may well be inevitable and potentially beneficial, but it doesn't follow that it's not dangerous. Plato himself was well aware of these arguments. He has Socrates argue in the *Republic* that 'philosophy must be wooed by true men and not bastards' (535c). He had in mind people who do not take philosophy *seriously* and precisely because of the potentially harmful effects of its irresponsible practice.

The text

Contrary to appearances, the *Apology* is a very challenging piece of writing.[19] It is at once a putative answer to the charges brought by the prosecution, an attack on the Athenians and on their justice system, and, the theme I have developed in the previous section, a defence of the philosophical enterprise. Socrates sometimes pursues these diverse, though not unrelated, aims simultaneously. For example, he assures the jury that he will speak the truth and so will not attempt to hoodwink them with rhetorical tricks (17b–c). This is intended to underwrite the testimony he is about to give, but at the same time constitutes a condemnation on the theatrical character of most trials. Juries expected a performance and professional speechwriters were on hand to produce a script for those who could not compose their own. Thus Socrates' remark holds typical juries in contempt of court. The tracing of the development of these various themes would require an entire book. The philosophical theme will constitute the focus of the following remarks, though we will pick up on one or two other matters of difficulty.

Socrates' defence of philosophy emerges from his discussion. He does not, for example, subject the claim that philosophy is just to elenctic scrutiny. His attempt to effect a change in his auditors' conception of his practice is conducted beneath the surface of his defence. With respect to this surface, we can divide the *Apology* into six episodes[20]:

- 17a–18a: the opening address
- 18a–23e: defence against the old charges
- 23e–28a: the cross-examination of Meletus
- 28b–35d: the divine mission
- 35e–38b: recommendation of counter-penalty
- 38c–42a: final addresses to jurors who voted for his acquittal and conviction

17a–18a

This passage has attracted attention because of Socrates' claim that he is not a 'clever speaker' and is unfamiliar with forensic oratory (17b; 17d). In the first place, Socrates proceeds to show himself familiar with forensic oratory; and in the second place, the speech is rhetorically very clever indeed.[21] What, then, are we to make of his claim? Some commentators have argued that the address is ironic: Socrates is, in some sense or other, asserting his cleverness. But against this he does not deny that he is a clever speaker under every interpretation of that expression: only that he will not produce a speech comprising the flowery language of a student exercise (17b).[22]

However, his true purpose in this passage is the assertion of the distinction between two kinds of speaking. Socrates discriminates speeches aimed at persuasion and speeches aimed at the truth. His opponents, he alleges, have spoken very persuasively: they almost succeeded in persuading Socrates, who believes himself innocent, that he is guilty (17a). The power of this form of speech, then, is not to be underestimated. Socrates is concerned that his truthful speaking will be mistaken for speaking unpersuasively: just as he would expect jurors to overlook the superficial differences between defendants' dialects, so he expects them to concentrate on the substance of his defence and not its superficial dissimilarity to persuasive speeches of his prosecutors (17d–18a).

In the background, here, is the distinction between eristic on one hand and philosophy on the other. Eristic is a form of rhetoric that aims at victory. The ability to marshal arguments successfully in the Assembly was a highly sought-after skill in Athens: the sophists professed to teach it and met the demand.[23] However, it was arguably the eristic, and not philosophy, that was responsible for the corruption of the young because it teaches the art of victory in speech and is bound by neither a respect for the true nor for the good. It is, then, in the service of whatever desires a person happens to have whether or not they aim at what is actually good. Socrates, on the other hand, is a philosopher.[24] As we will see, he represents himself as a seeker of truth about the fine and good. He has, furthermore, exhorted his fellow citizens to do likewise. Socrates' begins his defence by insinuating this distinction between eristic and philosophy into his speech.[25]

18a–23e

Socrates claims that before he answers Meletus' charges he must first defend himself against what he calls the earlier charges (18b). The puzzling character of this claim has, to my mind, received insufficient attention. Scholars have been willing to take Socrates at his word: a successful defence against the charges made by Meletus has been rendered almost impossible because he has already been found guilty of the earlier charges (19a; 18c).[26] But there are indications in the text that suggest this is neither his sole, nor his primary, purpose.

The earlier charges refer to a reputation Socrates acquired through the practice of philosophy. He provides two formulations of them:

> There is a clever man called Socrates who has theories about the heavens and has investigated everything below the earth and can make the weaker argument defeat the stronger (18b–c)

> Socrates is committing an injustice in that he inquires into things below the earth and in the sky and makes the weaker argument defeat the stronger and teaches others to follow his example (19b–c).

Socrates thus presents himself as charged with being a natural scientist and a teacher of eristic. Meletus charges Socrates with impiety and corrupting the young (24b–c). The charges are superficially disparate, but ultimately continuous. Socrates is going to claim that science is popularly thought to be impious and that Meletus believes he corrupts the young through his teaching (18c; 26b). Socrates can reasonably claim that a juror who accepted the popular view would be disposed to find Meletus' allegations credible. This is *the* obstacle Socrates must overcome if he is to make a successful defence. There are, however, some curious aspects of this passage that merit reflection.

In the first place the introduction of the earlier charges looks tactically dangerous: if Socrates fails to convince the jury that his poor reputation is unwarranted, he will have simply reminded, and possibly reaffirmed, the jury's belief in it. The risk involved is plain:

by his own reckoning his reputation, and not the prosecution's case, will be responsible for his conviction if anything is (28a–b). The significance of this risk, of course, depends on what he hopes to achieve, and Socrates is quite clear that he will not seek acquittal by any available means (39a).

Most puzzling, however, is his defence against these charges. Having built up their significance, their long history and their entrenched nature, one might expect a full-bodied assault upon them. But Socrates does little more than deny them. With respect to the charge that he is a natural scientist, he claims no one has ever heard him speaking of such things around the trading stalls in the *agora* (19d). With respect to the charge that he teaches eristic, he claims he has never taught anyone for a fee (19e). It is, of course, possible he anticipates that these comments will banish the deeply entrenched popular view,[27] but it is a noticeably feeble defence. We can imagine a juror thinking, not unreasonably, that the first charge referred to his investigating matters in the sky and under the earth and not what he talked about in the *agora*; and that the second charge referred to his teaching eristic and mentioned nothing about his doing so for a fee.[28]

The poverty of Socrates' defence compels us to question his motivation. Why would he refer to what he has discussed in the *agora*? And why would he stress his not having financially profited from his conversations? The reason is that he is trying to make the trial about his philosophical practice. He treats the earlier charges as if they pertained specifically to that activity and to nothing else. His insistence that he must answer the earlier charges before the later is, I think, a pretext that licenses his description of the origin and nature of his philosophical practice. One indication of this is that he devotes only a few lines to his denial of the earlier charges, but his description of his practice runs to three full Stephanus pages.

But why should Socrates think that philosophy is at the centre of his trial? He makes two points. He first claims that the earlier accusers, the authors of the earlier charges, are more dangerous than his later accusers (18c). The danger they represent is typically thought to consist in their power to determine the verdict with respect to the later charges.[29] But this is not what Socrates says: he claims his first accusers are dangerous because people who believe them go on to believe that a natural scientist cannot also believe in gods (18c). That is to say, they inculcate the false belief that philosophy is necessarily impious. Socrates' second point is that he stands accused of wrongdoing or injustice (19c; cf. 24b–c). In one respect this is unremarkable and is consistent with his presentation of his reputation in the form of an official indictment. None the less, he represents the earlier charges as implying that his philosophical activity contravenes the law.

Socrates' defence comprises both his explanation of its divine origins and his assertion that it is a good both for the individual and for the city. The first part of his defence brings us to the tale of the Delphic oracle (20e–23c).

Socrates claims that Chaerephon made the long journey to Delphi impetuously. He asked the Pythia, the priestess, whether there was anyone wiser than Socrates and she indicated there was not. Socrates was puzzled when Chaerephon told him her response, because he knew he possessed no wisdom either great or small. He decided to test the oracle to clarify its meaning. This led him to examine politicians, poets and artisans because they professed to know fine and good things. None of these men turned out to be wise. When Socrates' demonstrated their ignorance they slandered him, calling him a natural scientist and a sophist.

Even in this abbreviated form, the story raises many intriguing questions that have occupied scholars. For example, isn't the attempt to refute the oracle itself an act of impiety? If so, the very text of the *Apology* confirms Socrates' guilt. Scholars defend Socrates on this point by claiming that he seeks to refute obviously false interpretations of the oracle.[30] But it's not clear this answers the allegation: he submitted the oracle to rational scrutiny, and thus reason, and not the god, is his final authority. The question for us, however, is whether this constitutes an adequate defence of philosophy against the charge of impiety.

Socrates' strategy is clear: his philosophical practice was divinely commanded and so is not impious (21e; 23b). But on what basis does he claim the god commanded him to philosophise? Let's suppose that Socrates is justified in accepting as accurate both the Pythia's response to the question and Chaerephon's subsequent report of it.[31] Socrates then identifies the true meaning of the oracle on the basis of an inference. The politicians, poets and artisans all claim to possess wisdom, but they do not. Therefore, the meaning of the oracle is that no one is wiser than Socrates because he is aware of his ignorance whereas those other men are not. The god alone is wise and this human wisdom, the cognisance of ignorance, is of little or no value (23a). Socrates further claims this constitutes an instruction to continue testing all those with pretensions of knowledge, despite the enmity his refutations inevitably cause.

The problem is that Socrates' final interpretation of the oracle is descriptive but he treats it as prescriptive. According to his analysis, the oracle states how things are with respect to the distribution of knowledge. But the prescriptive claim that Socrates should continue testing people elenctically does not follow from this descriptive claim alone. Socrates, then, appears guilty of inferring an 'ought' from an 'is'. But while it's true that Socrates cannot validly infer a prescriptive conclusion from exclusively descriptive premises, we must of course satisfy ourselves that he tries to do so.

One compelling piece of evidence is Socrates' later claim that he received the divine command in dreams and in all the other ways such instructions are typically transmitted (33c).[32] But Reeve points out that Socrates already speaks of the 'god's business' before he mentions any such dreams.[33] He defends Socrates on this point by claiming that as a devotee of Apollo Socrates had independent grounds for establishing the truth of the god's pronouncements in the face of potential counterexamples.[34] However, Socrates nowhere states the time at which he received his instructions through dreams and this undermines the motivation for Reeve's interpretation, which requires us to make further assumptions about Socrates' beliefs. Nevertheless, the piety of philosophy hinges upon Socrates' receipt of a divine command to which he is the sole witness.

Thus far Socrates has distinguished his practice from eristic and has argued the former confirms his religious devotion. One could hardly claim the case was thus far compelling, but Socrates could improve its plausibility if he were to reveal why the god would command such a thing. He aims to do this by arguing that philosophy is an intrinsic good. But first comes his confrontation with Meletus.

23e–28a

Although Socrates' cross-examination of Meletus is worth close scrutiny, we will not consider it in any detail here. Its philosophical significance lies in two small points: that believing in gods is inconsistent with atheism and that Socrates could not have voluntarily corrupted the young (27a; 25e–26a). The first of these presents no special problems of interpretation and the second is an application of the principle attributed to Socrates that no one errs willingly (which we will consider in Chapter Ten). We will instead briefly comment on the cogency of Meletus' evidence.

'Socrates easily defeats Meletus in argument'.[35] This assessment of Socrates' cross-examination of Meletus is not uncommon. And although it is sometimes forcefully pointed out that nowhere does Socrates deny the published charge that he does not recognise the gods of the city, recently scholars have argued just as forcefully that, in the absence of statute, a defendant only needs answer the plaintiff's interpretation of the charges.[36] This effectively rescues Socrates from the allegation that he distorts the subject matter and secures a hollow victory in debate with Meletus.

On the face of it, Meletus' answers do seem embarrassingly bad. He cheerfully states that Socrates alone is responsible for the demise of the city's youth; and he fails to anticipate the contradiction he walks into by claiming Socrates is both an atheist and a believer in supernatural beings (25a; 27a). However, I will suggest here that he is to some extent a victim of his own incompetence and that his answers contain matters of substance.

Within the context of the dialogue, Socrates cross-examines Meletus as a witness to the charges he has made. Reeve argues that Socrates alleges Meletus irresponsibly brought him to court. The justification for this allegation is contained in the passage 25c–26b. I don't propose to examine Reeve's reconstruction of the argument, but instead to pick up on one point in it: Socrates asks Meletus whether he believes he corrupts people voluntarily or involuntarily. Meletus claims he does it voluntarily (25d). Socrates shows this is inconsistent with the principle that people do not willingly cause themselves harm.

But Meletus would have just listened to Socrates tell the story of the Delphic oracle, the outcome of which was his avowed belief that the god had commanded him to carry on testing the people of Athens. He thus knew what he was doing when he undertook his activity and openly acknowledges that the young men who attach themselves to him copied his practice. It is not then so unreasonable for Meletus to claim Socrates voluntarily corrupts the young.[37]

Meletus' second egregious mistake is his accusation of atheism. How, one wonders, could he not see Socrates' line of attack coming? But as far as Meletus is concerned Socrates innovates in religion: he invents or introduces new deities. Now, in ordinary life such a suggestion would likely be treated as a straightforward impossibility: how could a mortal man create a divine being? But if it is not possible for a person to really create a divine being, then Meletus can reasonably claim that Socrates is an outright atheist.

It does not, of course, follow that Socrates would have nothing to say in response to more carefully formulated answers. But there does seem to be a *prima facie* case here for thinking him guilty of, if not cheating, then an exploitation of his opponent's disputative incompetence.[38]

28b–35d

We return now to the issue of the good of philosophy we set to one side during our consideration of the evidence of Meletus. Socrates concludes that what has been said is a sufficient defence against the later charges (28a), but he continues speaking for a further seven Stephanus pages. (His defence to this point amounts to ten pages.) One might worry Socrates is in danger of introducing irrelevant evidence to the court. However, Dover points out that:

> [t]he question to which our own courts address themselves is 'Has the defendant done what he is alleged to have done?' … An Athenian court seems rather to have asked itself 'Given this situation, what treatment of the persons involved … is most likely to have beneficial consequences for the community?'[39]

Thus we should not imagine a modern jury frowning at a defendant for prattling on about matters apparently tangential to the accusations. Socrates appeals to the jurors' sense of what is best for the community by trying to persuade them that philosophy is the greatest good for humankind. Although he makes a number of important claims in the speeches that flank the jury's verdict of guilty, we will restrict our discussion to the consideration of just two: the suggestion that he should be ashamed to die for philosophising and the declaration that the jury should return a verdict of not guilty for their sake and not his.

Socrates raises the following question: 'Do you feel no compunction, Socrates, at having pursued an activity which puts you in danger of the death penalty?' (28b). This is a strange question, but Socrates' purpose in posing it is to create the opportunity to assert the supreme value of philosophical discussion.[40] He compares himself to Achilles and the heroes at Troy who gave their lives for fine and worthy causes.[41] But the comparison may strike us as preposterous. With the exception of his own tours of military duty, Socrates has spent his time challenging people to defend their way of life. War heroes, by contrast, plunge themselves into battle in the name of the right and the good. But Socrates' point is that he should be no more ashamed of finding himself facing death than any other person who acts for the sake of what is fine and good. Neither he, nor soldiers, should be ashamed at the prospect of death because they are acting for the sake of the good.

One problem here is that Socrates proceeds to say he doesn't fear death because that would be just another case of believing one knows what one does not (29aff.). He cannot, then, claim to fear without contradicting his earlier disavowal of wisdom. But his rhetorical strategy here hinges on his claim that the practice of philosophy is just (28b) and that one should risk *even* death for a just cause. The implication is that just causes, in this case philosophy, are as valuable as life itself. But if death is not something to be feared, the significance of this bold assertion would appear to be diminished. But this criticism is wide of the mark. For Socrates the sole criterion for the determination of action is its justice or injustice (28c). No one knows whether death is good or evil, and so Socrates disqualifies it from consideration when deciding whether to philosophise or not. He is not, then, comparing the value of philosophy against the value of death and determining that the good of philosophy outweighs the evil of death. He is isolating *the* standard against which we should appraise any course of action.

Socrates, then, has asserted that philosophy is just. The final point we will examine is his claim that it is the greatest good (38a): the philosophical life is the most pleasant (41b) and happy (41c) life for human beings. He captures the point in his memorable slogan that 'the unexamined life is not worth living' (38a). Since Socrates has dedicated his life to the practice of philosophy, it follows that his service is the greatest good to have been bestowed upon Athens (30a). He is quite simply a gift from the god (31a).

These are extraordinary claims that appear both provocative and arrogant. To unpick some of the issues here we need first to note what Socrates thinks his service to the city comprises. It consists in: (i) the exhortation of his fellow citizens to make caring for the health of their souls their first priority; and (ii) the elenctic examination of anyone who professes already to do this (29e–30a). But why should anyone suppose that (i) and (ii) constitute the greatest human good?

One suggestion is that the value of philosophy is instrumental. Philosophy on this account is in the service of life: it purges one's heart of errors that would lead one to have a poor and unpleasant life. The value of philosophy consists in its power to realise something that is good in itself, viz. a happy life. But while this may capture some of what Socrates has in mind, it looks vulnerable to objection. Philosophy would be of no value to a person who led a 'charmed life': a heart free from error would gain nothing from elenctic examination. But Socrates thinks that philosophy is good in itself and not just because of its consequences.

Tredennick, like many translators, renders Socrates' famous slogan 'the unexamined life is not worth living', which raises worries about the possibility of a false dichotomy. Is it, for example, really the case that a person who fails to examine his life is better off dead?[42] Bloom, however, provides an alternative translation: 'the unexamined life is not liveable for a human being'.[43] This brings out the sense in which philosophy is supposed to be integral to human life. Philosophical discussion itself is a source of pleasure (41b). It is, furthermore, a sufficient condition for happiness (41c). Commentators have agonised over the precise meaning of these claims. The sketch that follows reflects one way of understanding Socrates' meaning.

The unexamined life is the life of an animal. An animal acts out of whatever beliefs or desires it happens to have without appraising their significance or place in the broader context of life. They are, as Frankfurt famously put it, wantons.[44] But this is not the life to which Socrates thinks we ought to aspire: we have the capacity to reflect and evaluate and in the exercise of these capacities we realise our humanity. The defence of philosophy reaches its completion, then, in Socrates' bold claim that it constitutes the best life for a human being. But just how plausible is that? Richard Wollheim, for example, notes the phenomenon of malign self-examination, which precludes the commission of action because one is sunk in reflection.[45] We may also wonder whether the life of an unreflective person really is worse than that of Socrates. Or whether that simply reflects the prejudice of intellectuals to prefer debating and doubting propositions to the everyday business of work and following the football. Furthermore, people nowadays resist the contention that there is a single form of life that is genuinely best: there is a plurality of good lives. But, despite the high-flown rhetoric of Socrates' speech, the text does not imply that philosophy is the only good in life. A nurse and a banker can realise good and pleasant lives: Socrates' claim is that examination plays a constitutive role in that possibility. Our response to the grounds of Socrates' position remains speculative because he does not justify his claim in the text. We are left confronting a claim that philosophers and readers have found challenging since he made it.

Conclusion

In his essay on the *Apology* Myles Burnyeat records his asking his audience whether or not they would have judged Socrates guilty.[46] We may ask ourselves a similar question regarding the success of Socrates' defence of philosophy. It must be admitted that it is incomplete. He operates at a level of assertion and insinuation. The question that remains is whether this would be the character of any such defence, i.e. whether there is something inherent in the nature of philosophy that precludes a successful defence. But whether or not Plato intended it to be complete is another matter. To answer this we would need to identify its original readership and consider whether it would communicate enough to them about the value of the philosophical enterprise.

CHAPTER FOUR

Crito

Introduction

The *Crito* is among the shortest and most controversial of Plato's dialogues. Controversial because Socrates appears to defend an extreme form of authoritarianism: citizens, he says, are under an absolute obligation to do whatever the state demands of them. This is all grist to the mill for commentators such as Karl Popper who argue that Plato advocates totalitarianism.[1] But the position is distasteful to Socratic scholars of a more liberal disposition who believe that, under certain circumstances, civil disobedience is entirely justified. Perhaps unsurprisingly, then, we encounter arguments in the secondary literature to the effect that our obedience is not absolute or that Socrates does not endorse the authoritarian arguments of the second half of the dialogue.

Scholars have paid particular attention to what appears to be a contradiction between the *Crito* and the *Apology*. At his trial Socrates entertained the idea of his being released on the condition that he abandon philosophy; a proposal he rejected most forcefully (*Apology* 29c). He went on to refer to his refusal to comply with an order of The Thirty, when they were in power, to arrest Leon of Salamis (ibid. 32d). Both passages suggest that Socrates was willing to break the law if he judged it to be unjust. But the argument of the *Crito* appears to conflict with this: Socrates argues that he is under an obligation to obey all and every law of the state.

The form of the dialogue is distinctive. Although it includes familiar passages of question and answer, these do not result in the exposure of an inconsistency. It is not, then, formally elenctic. The dialogue also contains lengthy, and superficially unstructured, speeches from the Laws of Athens. These are largely rhetorical and are only occasionally interrupted for the sake of obtaining Crito's agreement. The reconstruction of that part of the dialogue presents the reader with a special set of challenges.

The dialogue is set in 399, about 30 days after Socrates' trial. The date of its composition is uncertain. Scholars traditionally supposed the *Crito* and the *Apology* were written around the same time because of the commonality of their subject matter. But given the uncertainly surrounding the dating of the *Apology* the thematic connection is of little use. The dialogue's authenticity has been doubted on stylistic grounds, but is typically treated today as genuine.[2]

The drama

Capital sentences in fourth-century Athens were typically executed immediately. The passing of Socrates' sentence, however, was delayed by one month because the day before his trial a vessel bound for Delos had been launched. The journey honoured the triumph of Theseus over the Minotaur and, for the entirety of its duration, Athens had to be kept pure. Convicted criminals such as Socrates could not be executed until the vessel returned (*Phaedo* 58a–c).

Crito visits Socrates in prison in the small hours of the day he believes the ship will return. There is an urgency to his visit. Socrates' friends have been trying without success to persuade him to participate in an escape. This is Crito's last chance: if he fails to persuade Socrates now, all (so far as he's concerned) will be lost. He makes a breathless and enthusiastic appeal to his friend; but Socrates declines once again. The dialogue concludes on a note of dispirited acceptance.

Acceptance lies at the core of friendship.[3] Part of the force of this dialogue lies in the uneasy resolution of a disagreement between lifelong friends. Crito arrives at the prison exhausted, anxious and depressed (43b). He finds Socrates sleeping sweetly and calm (43b). He is mystified by this difference between them: his reaction to Socrates' fate seems the more apposite. But the ultimate source of his disturbed state of mind runs deeper. Crito has, it would seem, been seized by a most troubling thought: the possibility that he does not understand his friend. Socrates' behaviour during and after his trial seems to him utterly perverse. He is failing to give proper consideration to his family, friends and even justice itself (45e). He has, moreover, apparently fallen in with his enemies and is now complicit in their plan to destroy him (45e). From Crito's point of view, Socrates is acting uncharacteristically, and this raises the unsettling possibility that he never understood him in the first place.

Beneath the surface here is the matter of parity in friendship. Crito appeals to Socrates to reconsider on every ground: he is prepared to risk his wealth and possible criminal reprisals for the sake of his friend's liberty. One can imagine his readily accepting Forster's famous remark that 'if I had to choose between betraying my country and betraying my friend, I hope I should have the guts to betray my country'.[4] Crito hopes Socrates shares his set of priorities, but his hopes go unanswered as Socrates proceeds to explain with great patience what he already knows: that justice is the sole criterion for the determination of action and that the principle of *lex talonis* ('an eye for an eye') is unjust. When reading the long speeches of the Laws, it's worth picturing poor Crito sitting there, broken hearted and crestfallen, as the steadfastness of his friend's resolve becomes clear.

None the less it would be wrong to think of Socrates as disregarding his friend. It has been suggested that Crito exhibits criminal tendencies in the dialogue and fails to recognise the force of law.[5] He intends to break the law and to commit an injustice. Crito himself admits that the life of a person with a corrupt soul is not worth living, so we can see that he risks far more than poverty and prosecution in conspiring to spring Socrates from prison. He risks the gravest thing of all: besmirching his soul. So, while it's quite true that Socrates neither tells Crito how much he loves him, nor how much his friendship has meant to him throughout his life, he does do what he judges to be right. He prevents his friend from doing wrong.

At the conclusion of the dialogue it is far from clear that Crito understands Socrates' motivation. There is certainly no indication that he appreciates his friend has saved him in what must have been the most stressful circumstances. But there is finally acceptance. He reappears in the *Phaedo*. He tends to his friend, he washes his body before the administration of hemlock, and it is to him that Socrates addresses his final words. Socrates' way of conducting his friendships is certainly unusual, but Plato's portrayal of this decisive and intimate moment between them is poignant for all that.

Obedience to the law

In one sense there is nothing shocking about asking why we should obey the law. The desire to make individuals stakeholders in the various institutions of which they are members sees even very young children, of four or five, being asked to reflect on why they should obey rules. But our familiarity with discussions of this kind obscures the shocking, if banal, implication that obedience to the law is not inevitable. This plain observation points to an important disanalogy between the laws of nature and the laws of a state. The latter, unlike the former, must in some way appeal to, or engage, the will of the individual. The typical form of this appeal is familiar enough: the laws of a state engage the will of the citizens on pain of financial, psychological or physical coercion. A person who breaks the law may forfeit his property or liberty. But a gangster may engage the will of a victim in a similar, if more extreme, manner. This raises the question of what, if anything, distinguishes the state's practice from that of criminals.[6]

The difference is that the state enjoys legitimacy where criminals enjoy none. We are obliged to act in accordance with the laws of the state because they are legitimate. We are not similarly obliged to obey a gangster and may reasonably oppose, with due force if necessary, his instructions. This seems correct, but what we want to know is in what the state's legitimacy consists. For it surely cannot exist in name alone. The force of this issue is visible in those circumstances in which it is most natural to ask we should obey the law: situations when the will of the individual conflicts with the law. There are, of course, various ways in which this conflict can emerge. The most obvious instances are those shabby occasions when people seek to profit by violating the law. But there are more problematic cases when a person's will is in conflict because of a matter of conscience. The journalist Donald Woods, for example, suffered prosecution in South Africa for having publicised acts of brutality against blacks. Ordinarily the rule of law trumps the will of the individual and the state is licensed to apply coercive measures to ensure compliance. The question is, what renders this legitimate?

One way to resolve the conflict between the individual and the state is to show that it is an illusion. The individual is confused and doesn't really want what he thinks he wants. He desires this or that because he judges it to be good. But he has made a mistake. If he could see matters as they really are he would change his judgement. The state here assumes a paternal role: its superior knowledge of what is good and bad makes it reasonable for it stops citizens wilfully injuring themselves by pursuing what is bad. But it is, of course, contentious whether the state is in possession of superior knowledge of what is good and bad.

Another way to resolve the apparent conflict is to relocate it. Superficially, it appears that the individual wants one thing; the law prescribes another. But matters may not be so straightforward. If the individual has promised, agreed or consented to the laws of the state, then the conflict lies between his earlier promise and his occurrent will. The legitimacy of the demand for the subject's obedience lies in his earlier agreement. The coercive apparatus of the state merely ensures that he honours his agreement.

But worries remain. If the individual's consent confers legitimacy on the state's demand that he abide by his compact, the withdrawal of consent would seem to negate its legitimacy. We can imagine an officer of the state pointing out that the legitimately binding character of the agreement survives the withdrawal of consent. The issue, though, is the source of this alleged legitimacy. The individual's consent cannot be the source of that because he does not consent. The binding character of the agreement must, then, enjoy an independent source of legitimacy. But now we have come full circle and return to the original problem of the sources of legitimacy. It seems, then, that we cannot account for the obligation of the individual to obey the state in terms of a contract forged between the two.

The text

The overall structure of the dialogue can be summarised as follows. After a short introductory exchange, Crito voices his desperate appeal. Socrates imposes order and establishes the sole determining ground for practical decisions. He then develops an argument through the rhetorical device of the personified Laws of Athens.[7] Although the brevity of the *Crito* permits exceptionally close readings, some of which turn on a single remark, we will try to retain some sense of the whole in the comments in this section.

43a–44b

We have already noted the contrast between Crito's state of mind and Socrates'. The other salient point to note is Socrates' report of a dream he experienced just before waking up. A woman in white robes appeared to him and said: 'Socrates, "to the pleasant land of Phthia on the third day thou shalt come"' (44b). Contextually this has to do with the arrival of the vessel returning from Delos. Crito believes it will come that night; Socrates' dream implies that it will arrive the following day.

But the truth of the dream rules out the possibility that Socrates will agree to escape: his decision to accept his fate has already been made. The decisive atmosphere is confirmed by Socrates' response to Crito's anxiety regarding what people will think about what happened: 'The most reasonable men ... will think that things were done *as they really will be done*' (44d). That is to say, Socrates will die in the manner prescribed by the court and that reasonable men will understand why that happened. The basis for Socrates' decision, then, does not appear to be, or at least not exclusively, the product of his discussion with Crito.[8]

44b–46a

It is a remarkable feature of the situation that even Socrates' closest friends did not appear to understand his motive in remaining in Athens for the passing of his sentence. This is, at least, the impression Crito's appeal gives us: the rapid multiplication of the counts on which he thinks Socrates should escape intimate an uncertainty regarding the true source of his decision to stay. The speech is realistically desperate and disordered, but we can none the less distinguish five reasons Crito hopes will move Socrates to consider breaking out of prison:

- Crito will lose an irreplaceable friend (unanswered[9])
- Crito and Socrates' other friends will acquire a shameful reputation (answered at 46c–48b)
- Socrates should not fear for his friends' property nor the possibility of criminal reprisals: it is just for them to help him (answered at 48c and 53a)
- Socrates, *contra* his remarks at his trial (see *Apology* 37c–e), does have places to go, such as Thessaly (answered at 53d)
- Socrates is being unjust with respect to himself and his paternal responsibilities (answered at 48c)

It's worth pondering whether these would be the reasons you would present to Socrates in this situation if you knew him at all well. It's hard to imagine the Socrates of the *Apology*, for instance, suddenly agreeing to flee having learned it won't cost Crito very much. We can, though, explain this in terms of the heightened circumstances: he hopes to suggest that there is every reason to escape (46a).

The appeal to justice, however, looks better placed to strike a chord with Socrates because he had been so concerned with it throughout his life. Crito argues that it is just for Socrates' friends to expose themselves to risk for his sake (45a). This enshrines the popular Athenian conception of justice as consisting in benefiting one's friends and harming one's enemies.[10] We noted in Chapter One that despite the searching criticism in Plato's writing, the popularity of this conception continues unabated. It's not uncommon to hear about people speaking, with evident approval, of wrongdoers 'getting what they deserve'. What is remarkable, however, is that despite his long friendship with Socrates Crito remains wedded to such a view. His intimacy with Socrates has not shifted his deep-rooted commitment to popular conceptions of right and wrong.

This underscores Socrates' contention that very few people ever will share his views (49d).

Although Socrates does touch on almost all the points Crito makes, he concentrates his response on the matters of reputation and justice. It is to these that we will now turn.

46b–48a

In this passage Socrates works to establish the conclusion that we ought not to worry about what people in general say, but only what the person who knows what is just and unjust has to say (48a). This is intended to answer Crito's point that both he and others will acquire a disgraceful reputation for having apparently prized money over friendship (44c). But it's not immediately clear that Socrates' conclusion, if he succeeds in establishing it, will meet the point. Crito's worry is that a bad reputation, however acquired, is harmful because people modify their conduct towards others on the basis of reputations. For example, a perfectly just and upright man may suffer torture and crucifixion on the basis of a totally unwarranted reputation for injustice (*Republic* 361e). Socrates himself, at his trial, claims that his renown for practising science and sophistry will, if anything is, be responsible for his conviction (*Apology* 28a). So, reputations do play a significant role in life and Socrates elsewhere acknowledges the fact.

But in his response to Crito, Socrates focuses exclusively on the truth or falsity of popular opinions and ignores the actions they may prompt people to commit. That would seem to be, however, beside the point. It doesn't matter that in point of fact you did not spill a person's pint; what matters is that the man is seven feet tall and believes you spilt his pint. There are, then, two separate issues here: from what kind of opinions we may learn something about justice, and the role of a person's reputation in people's conduct towards him.

Socrates is, of course, well aware that the people possess the power to imprison and kill him (46c). His argument is that that power is not decisive in practical deliberation.[11] In fact, Socrates claims that the condition of a person's soul is of the first importance (47e–48a). The soul is improved by just actions and is ruined by unjust actions (47d). The only opinions that have any bearing on what is most important, then, are opinions pertaining to justice and injustice. And although there is a spectrum of opinion about what is just and unjust, Crito agrees that we should esteem opinions that express knowledge of justice and shun those that do not (47a). The success of Socrates' response to Crito depends upon his successfully demonstrating his correctly assigning matters of justice as the highest priority. Crito has erroneously placed the avoidance of injury or death above the justice or injustice of the soul.

One worry with Socrates' argument is that by his own admission he has never met anyone who did know what was just and unjust (e.g. *Apology* 21d).[12] But that would not affect the claim that it is only to such opinions that we should listen.[13] A more serious objection is whether the condition of the soul is of decisive importance. This is, of course, a broad Socratic theme. But since Socrates has not denied outright the importance of friends and family, their relative weighting in our deliberation is presumably a serious question and not a foregone conclusion. What grounds does Socrates have for saying that there are no circumstances in which we should protect our family from harm or death through the commission of an injustice? He addresses this issue in the immediate sequel to this passage.

48b–50a

Socrates' conclusion is that it would be unjust for him to escape from prison. Since he and Crito agree that the question of escape amounts to a question of whether or not it's just (48b–c), Socrates ultimately refuses to escape. But how precisely does he go about securing this conclusion? There are two principal arguments Socrates develops through the imagined voices of the Laws. But these arguments are based on a set of action-guiding principles. In the present passage, Socrates obtains Crito's agreement to these principles. However, he begins by clarifying why considerations of justice come first in practical deliberation:

(i) Living well, and not merely living, is the most important consideration (48b)

(ii) Living well is living justly (ibid.)

(iii) Living justly consists in never willingly committing injustice (49a)

By the expression 'living well' Socrates has in mind *eudaimonia*, which is typically, though not unproblematically, rendered 'happiness' in English. For the Athenians, a person was *eudaimon* if he had the best life, by which they meant a pleasant, successful and worthwhile life. As students of philosophy we're likely to have encountered the notion in discussions of Virtue Ethics. But it's important keep in mind that *eudaimonia* is not a straightforward moral notion. We're familiar today with people who ruthlessly pursue their own ambitions to the neglect of their family, friends and obligations. We would not naturally describe such a person as motivated by morality, but we could fairly describe them as striving, however misguidedly, to be *eudaimon*. They are, after all, seeking to realise the best possible life.

Since the achievement of *eudaimonia* is the ultimate goal of all our efforts, it's not surprising that Crito readily accepts (i). His acceptance of (ii), however, seems less straightforward because, we might think, there is more to living a successful and worthwhile life than acting justly. We can imagine a person arguing for the place of pleasure, friendship, art and sport in the best life. This may look like Socrates privileges matters of fairness and equality over these other goods. But, in fact, justice here is a broad notion governing the place of all such goods in life. He is not, then, recommending a saintly role, but stipulating the minimal condition necessary for the good of any pleasure or art in life. We can trace something like this idea in the *Euthydemus*: Socrates suggests that a person is only *eudaimon* if he uses good things correctly (280e). It is, however, a striking thought that the ultimate basis for Socrates' decision to drink the hemlock is self-interest.[14]

We can now turn to the two principles that the Laws will rely on in following section:

(iv) A person must not do anything wrong, even in retaliation for a wrong suffered[15]

(v) A person must honour his agreements, provided they are just (49e)[16]

Socrates stresses that few people accept (iv). We can recall, in this connection, the popular conception of justice: benefiting one's friends and *harming one's enemies*. Although Crito says he accepts (iv), he readily violates it when Socrates invites him to specify the just cause Socrates has for striking at the Laws (50b–c). This serves to remind us just how deep-seated our sensibilities are: we can imagine Crito having heard (iv) many times before and yet, within minutes of assenting to it again, he acts contrary to it.

The other point worth noting here is that the obligation to abide by agreements is not absolute. There are, according to (v), circumstances in which a person is not obliged to honour his agreements. If, for instance, the agreement is unjust, then the parties are not bound by it. The significance of this will become clear in the next section.

50a–54e

We have already noted that this passage contains two arguments for the conclusion that it would be unjust for Socrates to escape. This is the view of several distinguished scholars.[17] But a first reading of the text can undermine one's confidence in this contention because, as the reader can see, the form of the speeches doesn't lend itself to straightforward reconstruction. The first section (50b–51c), for example, is predominantly composed of rhetorical questions only at the end of which does Crito give his assent. The significance of the issues raised, such as the parent–city analogy, is not adequately signposted. It is hardly surprising then that there are competing views about the character, and the number, of arguments in the passage.[18] However, two logically distinct sets of concerns do appear to emerge and scholars have tried to formalise these as arguments.[19] I will follow Kraut and refer to these as the 'argument from destruction' and the 'argument from agreement'.

Socrates raises a number of further issues in the section 53a–54d, such as how we will continue to speak of justice with integrity in Thessaly, but I will not comment on them in this chapter because they do not pertain to the justice or injustice of escape.

The argument from destruction looks like this:

(a) A person must not do anything wrong

(b) In escaping from prison Socrates would be violating the law that stipulates judicial rulings be binding

(c) The violation of that law would be wrong

∴

(d) Socrates must not escape from prison

Premise (a) simply enshrines principle (iv) to which Crito has already assented. Premise (b) looks straightforwardly true: Socrates would be acting contrary to the court's ruling.[20] The question, then, is whether (c) is true. The Laws claim that the law Socrates' escape would violate is fundamental to the entire system of laws and the state itself (50b). Thus the violation of it would constitute an attack on the integrity of the state. This may strike us as rather histrionic: surely a single violation of that law would not by itself invalidate it. Commentators typically explain this in terms of a generalisation.[21] If we treat Socrates' violation as endorsing the global violation of this law and if the Athenians then predominantly violated that law, then it's clear the law will have no operative force in the community. But, as Santas points out, there is, with the exception of the Laws' use of the plural 'judgements' (50b), no clear reference to a principle of generalisation appears in the text.[22]

An alternative reading is that Socrates would, by his action, be aiming at the destruction of that law and, by extension, of the state of Athens.[23] Rousseau makes the point vividly in *The Social Contract*: 'every malefactor by attacking social rights becomes on forfeit a rebel and a traitor to his country: by violating its laws, he ceases to be a member of it; *he even makes war upon it*'.[24] Although his lone action may not have the power of destroying the state, that is what the action would mean or signify. He would be effectively asserting himself as enjoying some independent source of sovereignty that would legitimise his attack on Athens.

But neither interpretation explains why the violation of the law concerning judicial verdicts would be wrong. We could argue that it would be an act of self-defence, especially in this case in which Socrates believes himself to have been unjustly convicted. If I strike at an assailant, I may inflict an injury, but it's not a foregone conclusion that what I've done is wrong. The parent–city analogy (50dff.) appears to supply the explanation here.

The Laws suggest that Socrates stands to them as he did to his father. Socrates was not on an equal footing with his father: he was not entitled to retaliate or answer back because he owed his being to his father. Socrates has a similarly unequal relationship to the laws. He must either persuade the Laws that they're acting unjustly or submit to whatever they command (50e–51c). However, the precise significance of this passage is not immediately clear. If intending the destruction of the state is wrong, then the parent–city analogy is superfluous because (a) forbids the commission of wrongdoing under any circumstances. If, however, intending the destruction of the state is wrong *because* it amounts to a strike against one's superiors, the analogy has some explanatory role but is not unproblematic.

The point is that the Laws themselves may dictate what is unjust.[25] They concede the possibility of this when they invite the citizen to persuade them that justice falls on his side and not the Laws' (51c). It follows that justice is independent of the Laws and that they, like citizens, are in subjection to it. The Laws, then, might enjoin citizens to do what is unjust. However, participation in unjust conduct is precluded by (a). Socrates does not dispute that the state is guilty of an injustice against him, and nor apparently do the Laws (54b). He disputes that that entitles him to retaliate. But, as Crito feared (45c), in accepting the court's sentence, Socrates is effectively colluding in the Laws' perpetration of an injustice.

The provision of the 'persuade or obey' clause is clearly intended to attenuate this problem. Obligation appears not to be absolute because citizens may attempt to educate the Laws by persuading them that their prescriptions are unjust.[26] But it must be said that the Laws remain sovereign and, if not persuaded, may demand obedience to their original directive.[27] It follows that a citizen, then, ultimately obeys the Laws both if they emend their directive and if they are not persuaded by the arguments put to them.[28] This, then, underscores those allegations of implicit authoritarianism in *Crito*.[29]

In sum, then, it would be wrong to violate the law concerning the execution of judicial verdicts because Socrates stands to the laws as he did to his father. He is, however, granted the possibility of appeal, though the Laws retain their sovereignty. Much will depend, though, on the Laws' assessment of the relative status of Socrates and his homeland. For we are owed an account of the superior intrinsic value of Athens that warrants what Crito believes to be Socrates' collusion in an injustice.

We now turn to the argument from agreement. Despite the contemporary popularity of the contractarian approach, we should not overlook how controversial it has seemed in the past. Thus Hume wrote that 'were you to preach in most parts of the world that political connections are founded altogether on voluntary consent or a mutual promise, the magistrate would soon imprison you ... for loosening the ties of obedience'.[30] With this in mind, we may now turn to the text where we find the first mention of an agreement between Socrates and the Laws in the question they pose at 50c: 'Did you agree to abide by whatever judgements the state pronounced?' The Laws return to the alleged agreement in 51c–53a. The argument they have in mind may be formalised like this:

(e) A person must honour his agreements, provided they are just

(f) Socrates agreed to abide by the laws

(g) Socrates' agreement is just

(h) In escaping from prison Socrates would be violating the law that stipulates judicial rulings be binding

∴

(i) Socrates must not escape from prison[31]

Socrates and Crito have already acknowledged premise (e) and we have provisionally accepted (h) above. The premises demanding scrutiny, then, are (f) and (g). We will first consider premise (f).

The Laws claim that Socrates signalled his agreement in deeds and not words. He chose to stay in Athens when he could have emigrated (51d–e). So far as the Laws are concerned, Socrates has entered into an agreement and he doesn't dispute this. But the acceptable media for communicating agreement are, of course, distinct from the character and terms of the agreement. And it is to these that we must now turn.

It will be worth pausing here to reflect on the constitution of agreements in general. An agreement is the result of an act through which two or more parties come to share a common view about what will be done or what is the case.[32] There cannot, then, be an agreement between parties if they do not share a common view. But the existence of a mutual understanding is not all there is to it. The Greek word for agreement, '*homologia*', intimates the forging of a promise, which implies a commitment to keep to that common understanding. So, although agreements can be legitimately dissolved, the parties concerned must be aware of, and must accept, the dissolution.

The putative agreement between Socrates and the state pertains to rules governing behaviour, including the administration of justice. In order for such an agreement to exist both parties have a common view of these rules and both must have made a commitment to them. The Laws contend that Socrates signalled his agreement by remaining in Athens having observed the rules governing the behaviour of citizens (51e). Thus the Laws claim, and Socrates does not dispute, that he shares this common understanding and is committed to it. This would not, of course, apply to all citizens but only to those who are aware and make the commitment.[33]

We then turn to premise (g), which is of decisive importance because if it is false Socrates is under no obligation to obey the law. However, Bostock claims that the Laws fail to defend the view that the agreement is just.[34] Instead, the Laws argue that the agreement was freely entered into. Socrates was neither deceived nor compelled to make the agreement, both of which conditions would render it illegitimate. Furthermore, they contend that Socrates enjoyed a perfectly reasonable timeframe in which to decide: he could have left at any point in his 70 years should he have found the practices in Athens uncongenial.

Although these points may appear superficially intuitive, they have elicited objection. Hume, for example, disputed whether all individuals do in fact possess the necessary resources to leave. If not, there is a sense in which an individual is compelled to continue residing in the state, and therefore his alleged consent is not freely given. He goes on to dispute the claim that there should only be two alternatives, likening the choice facing a dissenting individual to that of an abductee who finds himself at sea, who is told he's perfectly free to jump and swim for it.[35] This is especially distasteful when we consider those circumstances in which a state conducts itself clumsily, arrogantly and brutally. So, despite Socrates' believing it to be the case, it's not clear that staying put constitutes freely consenting to abide by the law.

The other point, recall, is whether the terms of the agreement are truly just. *Contra* Bostock there is, I think, one passage in which the Laws intimate that the agreement was just. They claim that 'we have brought you into the world and reared you and educated you and given you and all your fellow citizens a fair share in all good things at our disposal' (51c). This immediately follows the passage in which the Laws spoke very forcefully of a citizen's obligation to obey (50e–51c). The sequence suggests a degree of parity: the Laws do not simply demand his obedience; Socrates is compensated with his life, education and access to goods. Now we could very well dispute whether absolute obedience is a fitting return for those provisions, but it would, I think, be exaggerating matters to claim they ignore the issue altogether.

Conclusion

We have focused on Socrates' claim that escaping from prison would constitute an injustice. This is supposed to follow from some basic principles governing conduct and which ultimately owe their existence to the egoistic desire for a good life. While Socrates goes to his death without acting against Crito's beliefs, the points of the argument raise some of the deepest questions regarding the source of political legitimacy (48e). And with respect to these the *Crito* is far from the final word.

CHAPTER FIVE

Euthyphro

Introduction

It is not uncommon for students of philosophy to encounter the *Euthyphro* when studying normative ethics. The famous 'Euthyphro dilemma' can be used effectively to appraise the intelligibility of divine command theories of morality, which claim that an action is right if God commands it. But the interest in the dilemma is not limited to philosophers who seek to put divine command theories to bed. More recently, philosophers developing response-dependent accounts of properties have made effective use of the 'Euthyphro contrast'. In terms of that discussion, Socrates is a detectivist about value. He thinks our judgements about *p* are true if they accurately detect mind-independent facts about *p*. Euthyphro, on the other hand, is a projectivist, who thinks our best judgements about *p* are constitutive of the truth about *p*. However, while some of this work takes its inspiration from Plato's dialogue, the arguments go well beyond what is discussed by Socrates and Euthyphro.

However, the interest in the dilemma is perhaps in danger of eclipsing Socrates' wider discussion of the nature of piety. Indeed, we may wonder speculatively whether without its dilemma the *Euthyphro* would continue to exercise its draw on philosophers in quite the same way. One reason for this, no doubt, is the reported decline of religion in general.[1] According to recent polls, for an increasing number of people fathoming the true character of piety and holiness simply does not figure among their daily priorities. The study of the dialogue does not, then, promise to illuminate an aspect of such people's daily lives.

Dramatically, the *Euthyphro* immediately follows the *Theaetetus*, which is the first of Plato's five-dialogue sequence covering the events of Socrates' trial and execution. At the end of their discussion, Socrates tells Theaetetus that he must leave because he is due at the King's Porch to answer the charges brought against him by Meletus at his preliminary hearing (*Theaetetus* 210d). The assignation of the dramatic date of 399 is, then, quite straightforward.

The *Euthyphro* is conventionally thought to be among Plato's earliest compositions. That view is, to some extent, upset by Plato's use of the word '*eidos*' (form) when talking about the virtues (6d). This is one of the words Plato later used to denote the Forms, which developmental readings situate in Plato's middle dialogues. The presence of '*eidos*' in the *Euthyphro* has led some scholars to group it with the *Meno*, which is typically classified as a transitional dialogue.

The drama

Euthyphro is evidently surprised to find Socrates waiting outside the offices of the King Archon, the Athenian magistrate responsible for religious matters, because he knows that Socrates typically frequents the Lyceum, a popular gymnasium. His surprise quickly blossoms into nosiness and he asks what Socrates is doing there. Having learned of Meletus' indictment, Euthyphro points the finger at Socrates' 'divine sign'. Euthyphro is a priest or a soothsayer and responds sympathetically: he has himself been subject to ridicule in the Assembly when speaking of the divine. Then, with immense casualness, he tells Socrates he shouldn't give the matter too much thought and should simply meet the matter head-on (2a–3b).

Euthyphro is conspicuously keen to talk about his own case (3e). He is a zealous and self-righteous man and we get the impression that he takes pleasure in publicising his keen-eyed concern for what is right and good. Euthyphro is prosecuting his father for the murder of a day-labourer who was recruited to work on the family land on Naxos. This labourer got drunk and murdered one of the family's slaves. Euthyphro's elderly father was uncertain as to what to do and sent someone to find out from a religious official. In the meantime, he had the labourer bound and thrown in a ditch, where after days of neglect he died (4c–e).

Scholars have pointed out that Euthyphro's case against his father alludes in various ways to Meletus' case against Socrates. Meletus, recall, prosecuted Socrates for corrupting the young. This was visible in, for example, the conflict between the young and the old: sons turning against their fathers.[2] At his trial Socrates referred to the sophists who were renowned for enticing young men away from their families to study.[3] Euthyphro, of course, has turned against his father and is evidently corrupted by his religious enthusiasm and self-assurance. Plato's irony being that while Socrates was held by Meletus to be the cause of the corruption of the young, he is presented here as tempering the younger man's heady religious fervour. He thus emerges as one who heals the corruption rather than masterminds it.

Although there would appear to be an historical inaccuracy in Euthyphro's bringing his case – in fifth-century Athens it seems only a relative of the victim could bring a charge of murder – what is truly intriguing is Euthyphro's motivation in doing so at all. Given Socrates' amazed reaction (4a), it would seem that Euthyphro was not obliged to bring the case against his father. In fact, Socrates initially presumes the victim must have been one of Euthyphro's relatives, which would at least explain his action in terms of painfully divided loyalties. But the true origin of Euthyphro's action, however, is his fear of attracting *miasma*: 'It is laughable, Socrates, that you think it makes some difference whether the dead man was an outsider or a relative … your pollution [*miasma*] is as great as his if you live with such a person in the knowledge of what he has done' (4b).

Miasma is spiritual pollution or defilement. People associated with wrongdoers were vulnerable to such pollution purely as a result of their association. It was believed to be causally responsible for subsequent misfortune and disaster. Thus Euthyphro believes he is in danger of pollution because he knows what his father has done (4c). Thus Euthyphro privileges his desire to avoid misfortune above filial piety and brings his father to court. Somewhat distastefully he is able to present as honourable his ambition to cleanse himself: he is simply and earnestly abiding by the requirements of divine law (4e).

Euthyphro's fears of divine reprisals for his father's actions were not entirely without foundation. Although the gods of the Athenians were not wholly perfect, they were capable of intervening in the world. The full extent of this may strike us as rather surprising. We might anticipate the belief that the gods could engender natural disasters, such as droughts or plagues. But they were also believed to affect people's characters and could even determine the outcome of social interactions between people.[4] What fell outside human control was literally deemed to be in the lap of the gods.

Euthyphro's professed knowledge of divine law is the dramatic pretext for the philosophical discussion of piety and holiness. Socrates hopes to learn from him so that he can deny with authority Meletus' accusation of impiety (5a–b). Piety in Athens consisted in one's correct observance of, and participation in, public religious conduct. The Greek word '*eusebeia*' (piety) literally meant god-fearing. That fear or awe commanded an individual's daily prayer and sacrifices as well as his attendance at major religious festivals on the calendar. Religion for the Greeks, if it can be called that, was largely a public affair, unlike contemporary religion in the modern world, which is private and personal. Euthyphro fails to survive the *elenchus* and, according to one tradition, abandoned his case against his father.

Piety

The public discussion of religion[5] since 2001 has been greatly elevated by the contributions of the New Atheists. These academics and writers have published polemics, produced television documentaries and participated in numerous public debates about the nature of religion. Their efforts constitute an informal campaign to challenge the cosmological and moral teachings of religious groups. Whether or not their arguments are cogent, they have been reasonably successful in steering the discussion to what they think it should be about. For example, whether believing in God makes people behave morally and whether the physics in the Torah is more or less convincing than the physics of the scientific community. However, we may well wonder whether the New

Atheists are uniformly correct in their assessment of the terms of the debate. We can imagine a theist turning round and claiming that religion is ultimately about a way of life and not an account of nature of the physical world.[6]

These contemporary discussions bear on our sense of the significance of Socrates' discussion of piety. The fate of our interest in piety is bound up with the question of God's existence. If there is no God, then there is simply nothing to which we can duly honour and revere. This undermines the ground for investigating the appropriate character of that honour and reverence. So if we approach the *Euthyphro* with an existing scepticism about the existence of God, we have good reason to treat the discussion of piety as nothing more than a matter of intellectual curiosity. But this is to miss the point that piety itself is a response to a deeper issue that arises through our acknowledgement of the human predicament. That deeper issue is not dependent on the outcome of the question of the existence of God.

Human beings are limited beings. Cast adrift in a sea of causes beyond their control, they are subject to laws of nature that none of them ultimately can resist. They may, for example, be able to mask or retard the visible manifestations of aging, but for all that they will age, wither and die. Within the narrow boundaries of life, some of us will be successful and others not. The causal origins of our success or failure do not, however, lie completely within our control. I cannot, for example, decide to be a celebrated actor: the achievement of that ambition is dependent on others who are not subject to my will.

The human situation is at once alarming and thrilling. Fortunately, for those of us who cannot bear too much reality, the modern world is replete with salves for our metaphysical predicament: television, 24-hour news, fashion and politics all conspire to keep our eyes on the ground. But to turn one's eyes up to the sky at night leaves one in no doubt as to the slightness of life in the broader scheme of things. How, though, do we connect these reflections with the discussion in Plato? The recognition of the human situation forces upon us the question of how to respond to causes that affect us but which are out of our control. Hume captures the problem with characteristic force:

> We are placed in this world, as in a great theatre, where the true springs and causes of every event are entirely concealed from

> us; nor have we either sufficient wisdom to foresee, or power to prevent those ills, with which we are continually threatened. We hang in perpetual suspense between life and death, health and success, plenty and want ... These *unknown causes*, then, become the constant objects of our hope and fear; and while the passions are kept in perpetual alarm by the anxious expectation of the events, the imagination is equally employed in forming ideas of those powers on which we have so entire a dependence.[7]

One reaction is the religious one: we animate those powers, attribute to them a sensibility responsive to our efforts and beseech to them in the hope of cooling their fury. Another reaction is that of the New Atheists, who conceive of those powers as blind and indifferent to our lives. This leaves us with the responsibility to act in the best way we can (by our own standards) with straightforward acceptance of an unconscious death. Most ambitiously, we can assert our own causal efficacy and effectively do battle with those powers. The increasing popularity of books that detail mechanisms by which we can all become successful is indicative of an attitude of formidable defiance. Many of us, apparently, are not prepared to give up all that easily. Our situation in one respect recalls Pascal's declaration that everyone is obliged to wager with respect to the existence of God.

I will conclude this section with a personal reflection. I have in my adult life been struck by the number of people I have met who, though trenchantly opposed to the very idea of the supernatural, find a place in their thinking for the 'law of karma' or who use the expression that 'what goes around comes around'. They would, if pressed on the issue, dismiss it as superstition and their use of the expression an artefact of culture. But at the same time the propensity to reach for such expressions at all discloses the acknowledgement of the problem to which piety is one response among many.

The text

The question that drives the philosophical discussion of the text concerns the nature of piety or holiness. Although these might seem like alternative translations of one word, the text makes use of two different words: '*eusebeia*' (piety) and '*hosia*' (holiness). A person is *eusebes* if he reveres and honours the gods appropriately. Something is *hosios*, however, if it has been divinely sanctioned or approved by the gods. Piety in the first instance, then, has to do with an individual's assessment of the importance of honouring the gods and his ability to express as much in his actions. Holiness, on the other hand, has to do with the gods or what belongs to the gods.

Although in the fifth century Greeks did use the words interchangeably, the intelligibility of the dialogue requires us to remain alert to these differences in nuance. Euthyphro's third definition, for example, is that something is holy if it is loved by all the gods (9d). That looks like a reasonable account of what makes something holy, but is not transparently an adequate account of god-fearingness (piety). The translations I use here follow the Greek so that the reader may appraise the issue when it arises.

The dialogue comprises Socrates' examination of five definitions of piety or holiness. Euthyphro is, however, only exclusively responsible for the first two: the remaining definitions are more or less shaped by Socrates' interventions.

5c–6e

Before he poses his 'What is F?' question, Socrates obtains Euthyphro's assent to the claim that holiness is unitary. Holiness denotes a single property whose presence or absence across every sphere of activity is responsible for the holiness or unholiness of things (5d). Socrates doesn't flag up the significance of this point, but it is anyway fairly clear. By ruling out the possibility of ambiguity, Euthyphro will be committed to the production of a single definition of holiness.[8]

Euthyphro first defines holiness in terms of the prosecution of a wrongdoer for murder or for stealing from temples whether or not he is a relative (5d–e). He immediately justifies his definition by claiming divine precedent for it: Zeus imprisoned his father, Kronos, for swallowing his sons; and Kronos castrated his father, Uranus, for imprisoning his sons under the earth.[9] The reaction from his relatives has clearly got to Euthyphro, as he volunteers a justification for his claim that was not solicited. He is evidently concerned with whether or not he is in the right. People esteem Zeus as the best and most just god; but his family are angry with him for following Zeus's example (6a). When appraising Euthyphro's answers it's worth keeping in mind the extent to which this concern may control his responses.

Euthyphro's justification for his definition further reveals his commitment to a literal and superficial reading of poets. The irony here, of course, is that Euthyphro has asserted his claim to be an expert and an authority on religious matters. His use of poetry, however, indicates an entirely pedestrian and simplistic approach. He is, of course, not alone: we are all too aware today of people who treat scripture in this way.

Socrates' first question is about whether Euthyphro really believes that the gods are at war with one another and that there exists a state of enmity between them (6a–b). Euthyphro states he does. The examination of his first definition, however, does not depend upon this admission. Its significance is made plain in the next section of the text. But readers interested in Socrates' religious views should note that he implies he does *not* believe it. Although the Athenians did not possess scripture as such, which implies the impossibility of heresy, the works of Homer and Hesiod were fundamental to the cohesion of the society.

Socrates' response to Euthyphro's definition is straightforward. He maintains that it fails to meet the substitutivity condition (6d). We cannot universally substitute 'prosecuting a wrongdoer' for 'holy' in propositions about holiness *salva veritate*. For while it is true that 'consecrated ground is holy', it is obviously false that 'consecrated ground is the prosecution of a wrongdoer'. Euthyphro has, thus, failed to specify a property that is even co-extensive with holiness. The failure of his definition to meet this condition renders it inadequate.[10]

7a–9c

Despite his frequently alleged stupidity, Euthyphro appreciates the significance of Socrates' criticism of his first definition. He produces a definition that succeeds in identifying a property that is extensionally equivalent to holiness, but is nevertheless little more than a commonplace. He begins by defining holiness as that which is dear to, or loved by, the gods, and unholiness as that which is not dear to the gods (7a). The extension of what is holy and the extension of what is loved by the gods coincide precisely. It is paradoxical, to say the least, to suggest that there could be things that are unholy, or not holy, that the gods love and that that there are holy things the gods don't love. However, Socrates challenges this claim by exposing the contradiction between this definition and Euthyphro's earlier admission of disagreements between the gods.

Socrates begins by obtaining Euthyphro's assent to two apparently innocuous, but ultimately decisive, claims. The first is that the holy and the unholy are not the same. The second is that holy is the exact opposite of the unholy (7a). Socrates doesn't immediately spell out the significance of these points, but we can see that they rule out the possibility of the property denoted by the term 'holiness' having a contradictory character. If holiness were such an admittedly baffling property, Socrates' application of Euthyphro's admission of the enmity between the gods would not prove so threatening.

Socrates presents the following claims as inconsistent:

(1) holy = loved by the gods
(2) unholy = not loved by the gods
(3) x is loved by god_a and god_b
(4) x is not loved by god_c and god_d
(5) x is holy and unholy (from (1) and (3); and (2) and (4))
(6) holiness and unholiness are exact opposites

Proposition (5) states that one thing, x, is taken to be both holy and unholy, which (6) implies is impossible. Socrates proceeds to expose the full significance of (2) and (3), which imply either the non-existence of a standard of holiness or the limitations of the gods in applying such a standard (7b–e).

Socrates claims that people do not dispute matters where there is an adequate means of resolution. In mathematics, for example, we can settle a dispute about whether '2/3 + 2/5' is greater than 1 by recourse to arithmetic. Since '2/3 + 2/5' is equal to 16/15 and since 1 is equal to '15/15', we can resolve this dispute without descending into anger or enmity. This is not the case, Socrates claims, when it comes to value judgements regarding the just and unjust, and the fine and the ugly (7d).[11] We are perfectly familiar with disagreements of this sort. One politician declares a tax cut just, another denies that it is because it disproportionately benefits the better off. The dispute endures because of the absence of an acknowledged standard to settle the matter.

One possibility is that there is no independent standard of justice to which we can appeal. The use of the word 'just', then, would express the attitude of the speaker towards the object in question as opposed to denoting one of its properties. If that's the case, the gods do not dispute the presence or absence of a property of an object; they merely evince different attitudes towards the object. Another possibility is that there is an independent standard of justice but not even the gods have cognitive access to it. In that case, the gods' use of the term 'just' is intended to assert the presence of a property of an object; however, they, like us, do not know how to identify it.[12] The gods' assessments of the just and the fine, then, are either cognitively empty (because they're not about anything) or epistemically unreliable (because they're judgements originating from ignorance).

One might expect Euthyphro to respond by abandoning one of three things: his definition, his claim that the gods disagree, or his avowed commitment to the impossibility of one thing being both holy and unholy. In fact, he does none of these. Instead he denies the existence of a disagreement with regard to the present case, which for him is the prosecution of his father. To his mind this allows him to retain his account of holiness in the face of disagreement on other matters without committing himself to an absurd account of properties. However, Euthyphro's confidence is misplaced: although the gods may coincidentally agree that what he is doing is just, unless they do so on the basis of knowledge their consensus is of little value. Without knowledge, they are not authorities on what is just.[13]

Socrates argues that Euthyphro's response to his challenge is vulnerable to criticism. Euthyphro claims the gods will agree that a person responsible for the unjust death of another deserves to be penalised (8b). Socrates concedes that this is likely to receive widespread assent, but thinks the real point of dispute is precisely whether this is an instance of a person having been unjustly killed. He asks Euthyphro to provide a reason for thinking that in the case of his father the gods would be of one mind, but he proves himself evasive on the point (9a–b).

Euthyphro has certainly got himself in a muddle here and his claim to expertise in matters of religion looks highly questionable. (He's happy, though, to reassert his possession of it at 13e!) It might look like we can help him out: the assumption that gods really are at odds with one another, to which he assented at 6b, was responsible for getting him into this mess. Why not simply deny that? There are a couple of ways he could proceed: he could argue that the poets have misrepresented discord between the gods where there is none; or he could argue that the gods' grasp of matters is uneven, some know better than others. He could then claim either that the gods are, as a matter of fact, of one mind, or that one should privilege the gods that know over those that don't.

Unfortunately, both these alternatives spell trouble for Euthyphro. If he chooses the first alternative, he's asserting his knowledge of matters independent of the poets. If he chooses the second, he's asserting independent knowledge of the matters the poets dispute. But more troubling than both of these issues is the implicit assumption that the gods' views are *not* constitutive of justice and injustice, fineness and ugliness. There are independent matters of fact about which they may know or fail to know. If he were to make that claim, he would be contradicting his own answer, which was that the gods' love of something explains its holiness. These issues re-emerge in the discussion of the famous 'Euthyphro dilemma', which we will now consider.

9c–11a

Socrates is responsible for the formulation of the third definition; Euthyphro merely assents to it. The holy is what all the gods love and the unholy is what all the gods hate (9d). For those readers interested in tracing the dramatic thread through the dialogue, notice that Euthyphro's endorsement of this may well be predicated on his judging it a special case of the second definition. That is to say, he approves of this revised definition because of the co-extensivity of the holy and the god-loved.

Socrates then frames the famous dilemma: 'Is the holy loved by the gods because it's holy, or is it holy because it's loved by the gods?' (10a). The question appears to be neatly symmetrical but, as we shall see, operates with two different senses of 'because'. Tactically, of course, the question succeeds in rendering Euthyphro the learner and Socrates the teacher (cf. 5a): he is flummoxed and confesses he does not understand (10a).

As the reader will appreciate from having read 10a–11a, Socrates' line of argument is difficult to follow. This is partly down to a problem about rendering the text into intelligible English.[14] But even if that were readily soluble, the development of his ideas raises plenty of questions. In this section, we will begin by commenting on the destination before turning our attention to the route Socrates hopes to take to get there.

Recall the substitutivity condition (see p. 21) above. It states that if G is a definition of F, we must be able to substitute G for F in statements about F. Euthyphro has defined holiness as being loved by the gods. If that's true, we should be able to substitute 'is loved by the gods' for 'holy' in statements about holiness *salve veritate*. The conclusion of Socrates' argument is that this definition does not meet that condition.

Euthyphro must either claim that the gods love what is holy because it is holy or that the holy is holy because the gods love it. He picks the former of these (10d). But if the gods' loving *x* is constitutive of its holiness, we can't *explain* their loving *x* in terms of the holiness of *x*. For, while it makes sense to say that 'the gods love *x* because it's *holy*', it doesn't make any sense to say that 'the gods love *x* because *it's loved by the gods*'. That isn't merely a bizarre thing to say, it looks impossible. It's only true that *x* is loved by the gods because they love it: *x* comes to have the property of being loved by the gods at the very point that they come to love it and not before. But if 'is loved by the gods' is an adequate definition of holiness, we should be able to substitute one for the other without changing the truth-value of the statement. Since we cannot, 'is loved by the gods' is not an adequate definition of holiness.

That, then, is the destination. How does Socrates propose to reach it? He begins by discriminating verbs in the active and passive voice: for example, Tom carries Stan; Stan is carried by Tom. And we can see that Tom's carrying Stan is causally responsible for Stan's being carried. Socrates then, without notification, turns to a distinction between the passive participle and the third-person singular passive.[15] Stan is carried (= passive participle) because he is carried (= third-person singular passive) (by Tom). The passive participle indicates the condition of the noun (Stan) and functions as an adjective (cf. Stan is tall). A verb in the third-person singular passive is simply that form of the third-person singular that indicates the subject of the sentence is the patient, or sufferer, of the verb. In the sentence 'Tom carries Stan' the subject 'Tom' is the agent of the verb 'to carry'. In the sentence 'Stan is carried by Tom' the subject 'Stan' is the patient of the verb 'to carry'.

Socrates' point is that we cannot substitute these two passive forms for one another without affecting the truth-value of the sentences in which they appear. The form of the sentence in question is '*x* because *y*' where *x* represents the passive participle and *y* represents the third-person singular passive. Now, if we return to the terms of the discussion in the dialogue, we can see what Socrates is getting at. For while it's true that '[something] is loved because the gods love it', it's false that 'the gods love it because it is [something loved]'. Euthyphro has proposed that 'loved by the gods' is an adequate definition of holiness. But we can now see why Socrates thinks that can't be right. For while it's true that 'the holy is loved by the gods because it is *holy*' it is false that 'the gods love the holy because *it is loved by the gods*'.

We're now in a position to raise a question regarding the Socrates' use of 'because'. Although his original question looked neatly symmetrical, it's clear that the first instance of 'because' specifies the motivating reason for the gods' loving something; but the second instance specifies the logical cause of something's being in the condition of being loved. This immediately raises the worry that Socrates is guilty of the fallacy of equivocation. Cohen, however, rejects this allegation.[16] Socrates can generate the substitutive failure within one sense of 'because':

(a) the holy is loved by the gods because it is holy

(b) the god-loved is loved by the gods because it is god-loved

'Because' is used to specify the motivating reason for the gods' love in both (a) and (b). While (a) is true, (b) is false (because it confuses cause and effect). However, Cohen argues that Socrates is only entitled to infer that we cannot define holiness in terms of being loved by the gods if the gods' reason for loving the holy is because it is holy. But this in turn raises another worry: why didn't Euthyphro simply state that what matters is that the gods love *x* and not the gods' reason for loving *x*?

This looks like an intelligible response to the entire line of argument. Socrates asked what holiness was and Euthyphro (with some help) declared it was whatever all the gods loved. But let's suppose he had asked about the nature of love and Euthyphro had replied that love was an attraction to and disposition to care for something. There are plenty of things we might say about such an account of love, but precisely why such an attraction and disposition might come about would not be an obviously pertinent one among them. That is either an accurate or inaccurate account of love. It's another question how love comes about.

It's true that the issues are independent. However, it doesn't follow that, admittedly for different reasons, the origin of the gods' love of the holy is irrelevant to the discussion. To see this, consider the following two possibilities. It could be the case that the gods love what is holy for no reason at all: their love is effectively arbitrary and does not follow what is worthy or admirable. In that case, what the gods love is no index to what is valuable in life. This undermines Euthyphro's reference to the gods to work out what he should and should not do.

Alternatively, it could be the case that the gods love what is holy for a particular reason. But now it seems that what matters is the reason why they love what is holy and not the mere fact that they love it. The righteousness of Euthyphro's prosecution of his father will lie not in the gods' approving or admiring it, but in the reason why they approve of it. Euthyphro is already inclined towards the second possibility because he derives his principles from the stories of the gods. The basis of the gods' love is, then, highly pertinent to the discussion.

So, the third definition under consideration fails because it does not meet the substitutivity condition. It is furthermore a defensible way to proceed against Euthyphro, even if it is somewhat confusedly expressed.

11e–15c

This section comprises the discussion of the final two definitions of holiness. The first of these is that holiness is the part of justice that enables the gods to accomplish fine things. The second is that holiness is the art of prayer and sacrifice. Both definitions are developed through Socrates' explicit suggestions. But both definitions are of enduring interest. Plenty of people, and plenty of politicians, say they believe they're doing God's work; and many more people engage in petitionary prayer. However, despite their interest, the present discussion will be confined to a couple of closing observations.

The first is the unity of the virtues: the claim that the virtues are, in some sense or other, one. Socrates' suggestion that everything that is holy is just (11e) and that the holy is part of the just (12a) brings the unity thesis to mind. However, whereas elsewhere, notably *Protagoras* 329d–e, Socrates speaks of the virtues as like parts of a piece of gold (and so essentially identical to one another), here Socrates speaks of parts of virtue with different characteristics. Euthyphro suggests that piety (*eusebes*) is the part of justice specifically concerned with our relations to the gods (12e). The rest of justice is concerned with our relations to other people. So, the intimated nature of the unity of the virtue in the *Euthyphro* is not straightforwardly coherent with what we find elsewhere. We will consider this again in Chapter Ten.

The second point is that, if we construe the art of prayer and sacrifice as a kind of trade with the gods, piety seems to emerge as less fine and noble. Socrates characterises the practice as a form of barter (14e). But if that is correct, in observing divine law one is principally concerned with the achievement of one's desires and not the achievement of the gods' will. It doesn't follow, of course, that the object of one's desires will necessarily be oneself. The accusation needn't be one of outright selfishness. The point is simply that in being pious one is led not by the moral authority of the gods, but by the calling of one's own heart, which can be specified apart from the divine law.

Conclusion

Although Euthyphro proclaims his expertise to the very end, he has failed to clarify the nature of holiness and piety. Scholars do believe, however, that we can find within these discussions a Socratic account of religion.[17] But whether or not that is the case, the dialogue illuminates the human situation by exposing the deeper issue to which piety is but one response: our ultimate dependency on a world beyond our control.

CHAPTER SIX

Hippias Major

Introduction

Despite its engaging and amusing titular character, the *Hippias Major* is a puzzling piece of writing. First, the dialogue is ostensibly about beauty (*to kalon*), but the dialogue fails to clarify the nature of the beautiful. It is not simply that the discussion ends aporetically: the point is that, unlike some interpretations of the *Laches*, the *Hippias Major* does not intimate where Plato thinks the truth lies. Worse, several of the proposed definitions have been judged to be woefully bad.[1] Second, there are several respects in which the *Hippias Major* appears to be discontinuous with other pieces of Plato's writing. The arguments are felt to be unusually bad and Socrates appears to act quite out of character when he speaks of deserving a thrashing for having given a bad answer (292a).

Some of these considerations fuelled the debate sparked by Dorothy Tarrant in the twentieth century, regarding the authenticity of the dialogue.[2] That discussion involves, among other things, an appraisal of the reference to self-predication ('justice itself is just' etc.), which is, according to developmentalists, a Platonic idea. But the contention that the *Hippias Major* is a later dialogue sits ill at ease with the youthful and comic character of the rest of the work. However, although Charles Kahn maintains its spuriousness, scholars today generally regard it to be genuine.[3]

The dialogue is set during the Peace of Nicias, which was negotiated in 421. The textual clues for this consist in reference in the past tense to Gorgias's visit of 427 and the intimation that Hippias is not in town in his role as ambassador for Elis, which would situate it during those fragile years of peacetime. Regarding the date of composition, Woodruff argues that it was written c. 390.[4]

The drama

Socrates initiates this conversation expressing surprise at Hippias' long absence from Athens. Hippias was a prominent member of the sophistic movement. A minor, but not insignificant, indication of his stature is his appearance in three of Plato's dialogues. In the *Protagoras*, for example, Socrates describes him as sitting in the seat of honour (*Protagoras* 315c) and he always speaks of him in the most complimentary terms.[5] This is generally thought to be praise laced with irony, but what we know of Hippias would certainly justify his position in Socrates' stated estimations. The breadth of his learning was extraordinary: he was an accomplished speaker on astronomy, mathematics, genealogy, history, painting and rhetoric.[6] He was also the first person to compile a list of Olympic victors. That may sound a peripheral achievement, but ancient historians dated events in relation to specific Olympiads. We are, then, in Hippias' debt for our grasp of the historical order of events in the ancient world.

Hippias is in Athens to deliver a lecture on Nestor's advice to Neoptolemus. The delivery of lectures (*epideixis*, literally an exhibition or display) was an established part of a sophist's practice. But the subject matter of Hippias' lecture takes us to the heart of the drama of the dialogue. He has been asked to speak about King Nestor, who seeks to educate, or instruct, Neoptolemus, son of Achilles, about what is fine, noble or beautiful (*kalos*). This is, of course, precisely what Socrates and Hippias will discuss. The sophists professed themselves to be teachers of virtue and, indeed, Hippias claims *no one* knows better how to impart virtue than him (284a).[7] But there is an irony here. Nestor's advice failed: Neoptolemus went on to commit numerous atrocities, including the murder of King Priam.[8] Just as Nestor failed to educate Neoptolemus, so Hippias fails in his efforts to educate Socrates. But it is not clear that he is entirely to blame.

When the discussion of fineness first comes up, Socrates says that he was humiliated in a conversation with his 'friend' (revealed to readers to be himself at 298b) when he failed to define what is fine despite having cheerfully made pronouncements about what is and is not fine. His stated ambition is not to be so humiliated again (286c–e). Hippias, then, has every reason to suppose that what Socrates wants from him is instruction in eristic, the ability to succeed in a verbal contest against this man.[9] His comments throughout the dialogue bear this out: he speaks of answers that no one could contest (288a) and answers that will confound Socrates' 'friend' (289e). Hippias is given to appreciate, then, that Socrates' first concern is not an inquiry into the nature of fineness. Furthermore, Socrates does nothing to disabuse Hippias of his misconception of his real interest. He could have said: 'Look, Hippias, I'm not worried about silencing this man. I want to know the truth'.

It is, of course, noteworthy that Hippias conceives of these sorts of situations in terms of eristic. Plato is often presented as intending to contrast eristic with philosophy. But as I suggested earlier (pp. 8–9), he did not think the sophists themselves were responsible for the desire to become accomplished in argument. That was a wider social issue, which the sophists exploited to commercial success.

These remarks about the speakers' failure to arrive at an adequate definition raise questions about the accuracy of some of the assessments scholars have made about Hippias. Alfred Taylor refers to him as 'childish' and notes his commission of 'elementary blunder[s]'.[10] Charles Kahn, who maintains the dialogue is inauthentic, simply describes the character as 'stupid'.[11] These assessments render Socrates' complimentary remarks at best ironic, if not straightforwardly dishonest. It's reasonable to suppose Plato intends to contrast the two characters: Hippias is attractive, polymathic, wealthy and boastful, whereas Socrates is ugly, ignorant, poor and self-deprecating. But it's not clear that he wishes his readers to take away an entirely negative conception of the sophist.

Scholars have speculated about the dramatic connection between the *Hippias Major* and *Minor*. The lecture Hippias refers to in our dialogue is thought, by some scholars, to have just been completed in the shorter work. Despite what is often referred to as a humiliating experience for Hippias, this reading would suggest the man to be rather thick skinned. He returns for more of the same two days later.

Beauty in action

Moral philosophers are apt to characterise morality in terms of obligations. Moral judgements can be thus distinguished from advice because the recipient of advice is under no obligation to follow it. Each of us is free to make his own bed. But according to some philosophers, the same is not true of morality: the subject is obliged and required to do what morality demands. This is, of course, felt to be a very good thing because otherwise acting in accordance with morality would (apparently) be left to the whim of the individual. Since morality is concerned with matters of the greatest importance, such as prohibitions of violence, we understandably seek something akin to a guarantee to the effect that this is how things will be done. The obligatory character of morality is intended to meet this desire: people have, as we sometimes say, 'no choice' about whether or not to do what morality requires.

Kant is perhaps most closely associated with this way of thinking. He thought that a morally praiseworthy person acts with a good will and that a person has a good will if he acts for the sake of duty. This means that the person is motivated to act because he is under an *obligation* to act and not because he happened to be *inclined* to do it out of, say, a desire to be nice or appear popular.[12] The obligation in question is categorical. But Kant is far from alone. On the other side of the aisle, Mill claimed that we are under an obligation to maximise happiness and to minimise unhappiness. We are bound to assess what we do in terms of its contribution towards happiness and unhappiness.[13]

But while the idea of a guarantee of safety might appeal to us, the picture of morality that emerges is not altogether congenial. Indeed, Richard Wollheim reached for the word 'nightmare' to describe it and we can, to some extent, see why.[14] Morality confronts us; it is prescriptive; it robs us of our knowledge of our actual inclinations towards what is good; it is thankless; and it demands perfection.[15] The binding claims of morality are, moreover, effortlessly acquired.

Christine Korsgaard uses the example of a person calling out your name while you're out walking. You are, she claims, immediately placed under an obligation to stop.[16] The emphasis of morality upon obligation and blame prompted Bernard Williams to liken it to slavery, the so-called peculiar institution.[17]

But we can over-emphasise the obligatory character of morality. Consider the following personal example. Well into her eighties, my grandmother used to volunteer for a local blind club. She would accompany the visually impaired on all sorts of trips. One such trip was to Calais. While there she slipped on the pavement and broke her hip. A young French woman called Charlotte, seeing what had happened, came to her assistance. She stayed with my grandmother while she waited for an ambulance and went with her to hospital (despite her having been on the way to work). My grandmother, it turned out, was going to be in hospital (overseas) for several days. Charlotte met my mother at Calais the next day and took her to see my grandmother. When my mother asked if she would help her find somewhere to stay, Charlotte simply gave her the keys to her flat. Charlotte's actions were, I submit, admirable, inspiring, energising, beautiful. When my father heard what had happened he remarked that 'there really are angels on the earth'.

One might object, of course, that Charlotte was under an obligation to act as she did, or perceived herself to be. But this is to divest her actions of those distinctive qualities that merit, to my mind, the epithet 'beautiful'. She freely gave of her time, money and home to perfect strangers: she *wanted* to do what she did; she was drawn towards it, as we are drawn towards beautiful things. When, moreover, we encounter admirable and beautiful actions we contemplate and marvel at them. This is beauty in action.

The contrast, then, with the picture of morality we started with should be clear. On the one hand we have a system of morality expressed in terms of obligations and requirements. Morality figures as a set of rules that must be obeyed. On the other we have actions that are performed freely and are expressive of individuals' evaluation of what is valuable and worthwhile. Here a person gladly undertakes to do what is good because it is precisely what he wants to do.[18] If, however, we conceive of morality exclusively in terms of obligations we are at a loss as to what to say about people like Charlotte.

The text

The philosophical discussion of the *Hippias Major* falls neatly in two. Socrates seeks a definition of the fine (*to kalon*): in the first half, it is Hippias who provides the definitions, in the second, Socrates. As the reader will see, the property under investigation, *to kalon*, can be intelligibly applied to a very broad range of things. In the first epagoge (288b–e) it is agreed that girls, horses, lyres and pots can all be *kalos*. And a couple of pages later Hippias suggests it is *kalos* to have accumulated wealth and to have buried one's parents well (291d–e). Unlike the *Euthyphro*, for example, in which we have an existing familiarity with the subject matter, the *Hippias Major* presents us with a distinctive challenge regarding what it is supposed to be about. Now, obviously one would hope that our sense of the nature of *to kalon* would be shaped by the discussion. None the less, it will be as well to have some sense of the common Athenian usage before we get started. This is particularly important for readers interested in other aspects of Greek philosophy: according to Aristotle, for example, virtue is undertaken for the sake of *to kalon*.

In the first instance the Greek word is applied to a person's visual appearance. A *kalos* man or woman was handsome or beautiful: good-looking and shapely. In its extended use, however, '*kalos*' could be used to describe actions and behaviour. In such cases the most natural English words to reach for are 'noble' and 'admirable'. These two applications do have something substantially in common: the sense in which we can stand in awe of things. But the word can also be used to signify basic praise and even affirmation. For example, Crito responds to Socrates with the single word '*kalos*' (*Crito* 47a). Fowler and Grube render this 'It is' while Tredennick translates it 'Fair enough'.

Throughout the dialogue both Waterfield and Woodruff use the translations 'fine' and 'fineness'. We will follow their practice here to keep in mind the single property in question. However, the reader is advised to keep in mind the tremendous breadth of the Greek term and how it might be otherwise rendered in English.

Interestingly, although commentators are quick to point out the poverty of Hippias' contributions, modified versions of them reappear in the second half of the dialogue. Hippias does try to capture both the visual and the extended senses of '*kalos*', without apparent success. But given the trouble contemporary philosophers in aesthetics have with the concept of beauty, we should perhaps not be too quick to join the chorus of disapproval regarding Hippias' efforts.

285c–293c

In this section we will consider Hippias' definitions of fineness. Socrates first obtains Hippias' agreement to the claim that there is such a thing as fineness and that it is thanks to this entity that fine things are fine. As well as committing Hippias to the claim that there is something whose nature they can investigate, Socrates insinuates into the conversation the claim that fineness is one thing. That is, fineness does not denote a disjunction of distinct properties. As we shall see, Hippias does not recognise this point, or, if he does, does not apply it in his answers to Socrates.

Hippias' first response to Socrates' request for a definition of fineness is that a 'fine-looking girl is a fine thing'. Robin Waterfield denies that Hippias intends this as a definition at all: it is, he thinks, intended as an example.[19] Paul Woodruff claims that Hippias is trying to trivialise Socrates' question.[20] I have already indicated above that Hippias does not appear to be participating in a search for the nature of fineness at all: he consistently speaks of confounding or silencing Socrates' opponent. However, Socrates *treats* his first response as a definition: he asks whether this is the property thanks to which all fine things are fine. Hippias misses the point. He understands Socrates to have raised a different question: whether a fine-looking girl really is fine (288b).[21]

Socrates overlooks the most obvious objection. Hippias has included the *definiendum* in the *definiens* and has therefore produced a trivial definition. He is more concerned with whether such a property meets the explanatory condition, which adequate definitions must meet (see pp. 21–22). Plainly, the beauty of a fine-looking girl does not explain the beauty of a pot or that of a mare. Alexander Nehamas suggests that Hippias believes he has specified a general, though not universal, sufficient condition for the fineness of something. This, for Nehamas, explains Hippias' failure to appreciate the significance of his concession that a fine mare is a fine thing too.

Hippias' reply does not meet the substitutivity condition either. For while it might be true that 'that mare is *fine*' it is certainly not true that 'that mare is *a fine-looking girl*'. However, Socrates doesn't get a chance to argue for this because Hippias points out that the fineness of girls and mares belongs in a different category to the fineness of pots (288e). The point of his qualification is not explicitly stated, but Hippias is evidently sensitive to the pressure Socrates is putting on the word '*kalos*'. The reason why it's reasonable to describe Socrates' pot as fine is because of its utility: it's well made, appropriately fired and holds a decent amount of fluid. But these considerations are quite different to what we have in mind when we think of a beautiful person. However, while this is true, Hippias doesn't recall that he earlier committed himself to the claim that there is an entity, fineness, responsible for the fineness of fine things.

Socrates uses Hippias' point to reject the claim that his first answer specifies a sufficient condition for fineness. Since a fine pot will be ugly compared with a fine-looking girl or an Elean mare, so a fine-looking girl will be ugly compared with a god. Therefore, it could be true that something is a fine-looking girl and yet false that it is fine (when compared to a god). Socrates seeks the property, the fine, the presence of which is responsible for the fineness of all fine things.

Hippias learns from the treatment of his first definition. In order to silence Socrates' friend, Hippias believes he must produce an answer that denotes a property with two distinctive features. The first is that it must be superlatively fine. This will block any attempts the friend makes to show that under some comparisons the property is ugly. The second feature is that the addition of this property to something renders it fine. This will meet the explanatory condition of an adequate definition because the presence of this property will explain the fineness of fine things. His second response to Socrates' 'What if F?' question is that gold is the fine (289e). Hippias explicitly states that this response meets the explanatory condition because the addition of gold makes even what is ugly fine (ibid.). And, although he doesn't say so, we can imagine his thinking he's struck upon something superlatively fine: gold was long prized as the most valuable metal.

Socrates treats this response as a definition and uses his secondary questions to plant doubts about whether the presence of gold is necessary for the fineness of fine things. Before we consider that point, however, it's worth pointing out that Hippias has specified a substance and not a property. Substances are the bearers of properties: gold has the properties of, for example, having 79 protons and appearing yellowish under normal conditions. Fineness, however, is a property of things: girls, mares, lyres and pots can be fine.[22]

Once again the definition fails to meet the substitutivity and explanatory conditions of an adequate definition. Socrates suggests that gold is not a necessary condition for fineness because the sculptor Pheidias knows what is and is not fine and he used ivory for the eyes of Athena. So either Pheidias, counterfactually, doesn't possess knowledge of the fine or gold is not fineness (290a–b). Hippias is reluctant to make either claim: he simply points out that ivory too is fine when used appropriately or fittingly (290c). His second response has in its original form, then, been abandoned: he now endorses a modified version, viz. that gold and ivory are fine when appropriate (290d). Socrates later suggests appropriateness as a definition of the fine, but here he proceeds to examine the claim that ivory and gold are fine when they are appropriate.

The point of Socrates' subsequent examination of Hippias' modified definition is obscure (290dff.). Hippias admits that there are circumstances in which gold is not appropriate. Gold is not, for example, an appropriate material out of which to make a ladle for soup. But since Hippias has already admitted this (ivory, and not gold, was appropriate for Athena's eyes) one might wonder why Socrates poses the same question again. The issue now, however, is not about whether or not gold is appropriate for this or that, but whether something could be fine even if it was not appropriate to make it out of gold. That is to say, Socrates tests whether the revised definition specifies a necessary condition for fineness. If Hippias has identified a necessary condition, when it's false that gold is appropriate, it must be false that the object is fine. But in this case, the wooden ladle is fine.

Hippias' first two responses are demonstrably inadequate as Socratic definitions of the fine. Vlastos characterised them as the 'goofiest' in the Platonic corpus.[23] But we should not, I think, dismiss them altogether. Hippias has, to my mind, drawn attention to features of fineness that a successful definition should capture. In the first place, fineness is not merely a reaction to an object:

there's a difference between liking something (for whatever reason) and judging something to be fine. In the second place, fineness is attractive, valuable and admirable. We cannot call something fine that fails to command our attention. These ideas emerge in Socrates' own suggestions in the latter part of the dialogue. So, although formally Hippias is not delivering an adequate definition his intuitions about fineness are reasonable.

Hippias' third response is formally no better off than his previous two suggestions. He tries to produce a sufficient condition for fineness. The fine is, he maintains, a good life (291d–e). This incorporates the accumulation of wealth, the enjoyment of health and demonstrably respectful relationships with one's family. Hippias cannot imagine anyone denying that such a life is fine. It's possible that that's true (though Socrates' secondary questions suggest otherwise), but nothing follows about the necessity of meeting such a condition for something to be fine. Even if we restrict ourselves to the examples of fineness so far considered (girls, mares, lyres, pots, gold and ivory), we cannot explain their fineness with reference to their possession of a good life.

Socrates' approach, however, is to question the sufficiency of Hippias' response. If it were, then whatever meets the condition must be fine. Socrates asks whether it would be fine for Achilles to bury his parents in a respectful manner (293a).[24] Hippias claims the suggestion is profane. But it follows that this definition does not specify that which is universally fine (293b). There are cases in which it may be true that something has lived the life Hippias outlines, but false that it is fine. We might wonder whether we could modify this definition to the effect that fineness consists in living the life appropriate to your kind. This would allow Hippias to retain something like his original proposal but would not commit him to the claim that it would be fine for Achilles to bury his parents. But this would still fail to explain the fineness of lyres and pots. What Hippias needs to do is to isolate what it is about such a life that makes it fine. In the latter part of the dialogue, Socrates applies himself to this point.

293d–294e

As we have mentioned above, in the latter part of the dialogue Socrates imagines his friend putting forward candidates for appraisal, and on each occasion easily wins Hippias' assent (293e; 295e; 296e; 298b). But it doesn't follow that Hippias has revised his conception of the purpose of the discussion. If that's the case, it might explain both Hippias' agreement with the suggestions and his complaint at the end of the dialogue that the unnamed friend is hair-splitting. If what is required is a definition amenable to the person who criticised Socrates, the critic is likely to favour his own definitions. Conceding will allow the discussion to move on. It is, however, likely to seem perverse for the critic to reject his own preferred ideas, which may partly explain Hippias' bafflement at his conduct.

Socrates begins by reprising the idea that appropriateness, or fitness, might be fineness. This looks like a reasonable suggestion. In the nineteenth century Edmund Burke took the idea seriously enough, although he concluded that fitness was not the formal cause of beauty.[25] Hippias endorses the definition and agrees to examine it with Socrates (293e). Interestingly, the question they purport to investigate is not whether appropriateness is fineness, but what appropriateness is (293d). This would appear to be at odds with what comes next. Socrates proceeds to ask whether appropriateness is responsible for a thing's appearing fine or being fine (294a). But an answer to this question will not tell us what appropriateness is, only whether it's constitutive of the appearance or being of fine things.

Another oddity is that Socrates does not explore all the options. He invites Hippias to say whether appropriateness causes the appearance or being of fineness. Hippias eventually asserts that it is responsible for both. But Socrates does consider whether appropriateness is the cause of being fine and not appearing fine. After all, this would seem to be the most straightforward response: there are numerous vagaries affecting a person's judgement about whether or not something is fine; ignorance of its nature being chief among them.

We can clarify both these issues when we recall that Hippias and Socrates have in mind a narrower conception of appropriateness than we might at first consider. It is something we would appraise visually. So, the appropriateness of ivory for the eyes of Athena consists in the visually appreciable effect. This explains what lies behind Socrates' approach. He wants to know whether appropriateness itself is a property of experience or of the object.

So he is, after all, concerned with the nature of appropriateness. Now, *prima facie*, appropriateness would seem to be a property of experience: a person judges something to be appropriate because he experiences it as such. It is this intuition Hippias seeks to respect when he says that appropriateness is the cause of the appearance. This interpretation also explains why Socrates doesn't consider the possibility that appropriateness is the cause of being fine and not appearing fine. We cannot, on the face of it, make sense of the idea of something being beautiful that does not look beautiful.

The truly suspect aspect of Socrates' treatment of the issue is that he does not consider the possibility that being consists in appearing.[26] That is to say, if something appears to be beautiful, it is beautiful. Although this is far from being unproblematic, the idea that beauty is in the eye of the beholder is a substantial position in this discussion. It is, however, something Socrates ignores.

Socrates argues that if appropriateness is responsible for the appearance of fineness, then it is not the property they're trying to identify (294d). However, if it is responsible for being fine but not appearing, then we have to explain the appearance of fineness in terms of something else (294e). We may be tempted to say, well why not? But then we must remember that Socrates and Hippias are thinking about visible beauty. It seems unintuitive to explain the fine appearance of a thing in terms of properties that are not fine.

At this point Hippias expresses some dissatisfaction at the format of the discussion. He feels that if he had some time to think he might be able to produce an adequate answer. In one respect this looks like a dramatic detail: Hippias is not used to feeling that he's out of his depth and he would prefer to prepare in advance, as he did in Sparta (285d–e). But his remarks also draw attention to what readers may feel is a flaw in Socrates' approach. The final word on the definition of fineness in terms of appropriateness was that they had not identified what they set out to find. But why the rush to move on to an entirely new definition? Those scholars who think Socrates believes he refutes propositions have a ready explanation: so far as he's concerned the definition is incorrect. But if we accept this interpretation, we're forced to credit Socrates with an innocence over the poor nature of his argument and a lack of interest in trying to see whether appropriateness is merely something that can be fine or whether it is an ingredient of fineness itself.

295a–297d

Socrates now proposes they examine the claim that usefulness is fineness (295e). The definition chimes with some of the examples they have already considered. When we describe a well-made pot as fine, for example, we may be referring to its usefulness. However, we can see that it doesn't naturally explain fineness of a young woman. One might try to construe this is in terms of fulfilling a need, but that is not obviously plausible.

Having introduced the definition, Socrates immediately analyses usefulness in purely descriptive as opposed to partially normative terms. He switches from the useful (which implies a positive value) to the capable (which carries neither a positive nor a negative evaluation).[27] This move only constitutes a problem if Hippias were to withdraw his endorsement of the definition on that basis. Hippias, however, is perfectly happy to accept Socrates' analysis, and so fineness is treated in terms of ability. The question, though, is whether Hippias should accept it. Although it's possible to construe usefulness in terms of ability to perform a function, that sits poorly with fineness, which, as we suggested above (p. 90), is an admirable quality, something we take pleasure in contemplating. That is plainly not the case with anything that is merely a capacity.

Hippias eventually realises this and suggests a qualification: that something is fine if it is capable of producing what is good. This reintroduces the normative component. We might be concerned that it is not the capacity to produce what is good that matters, but its actually producing it. Socrates' examination originates in this thought and he concentrates on the metaphysics of causation. He argues that, if the fine is the cause of the good, then the fine is not good because an effect cannot be the logical cause of itself. However, the force of this point depends upon our accepting both that the fine is good (which is agreed at 297c) and that the goodness of the fine is the good it is alleged to have produced. It is not, however, clear that we need to accept this latter claim: what is fine may be good without its being goodness, which Socrates treats it as producing.[28]

298e–303d

The final definition to be scrutinised is that fineness denotes that which gives us visual and auditory pleasure (298a). This recalls Hippias' original definition of fineness as a fine-looking girl. Beautiful people are pleasant to behold. The first point to note is the ground for the restriction of fineness to these pleasures in particular. There are some sources of pleasure that are contemptible, such as sexual pleasure. This may strike the modern reader as surprising: the popular view is that Greeks enjoyed uninhibited sex lives. But this misses the point. Socrates' friend here concedes that sexual intercourse is undoubtedly pleasant: the question is whether it is contemptible in appearance. One thinks here of Iago's fabulously unpleasant image: the beast with two backs.[29] Dover further notes that it was considered fitting for married couples to conduct their sex lives at home and that it was shameful to do so outdoors.[30]

So, Socrates may have reasonable grounds for restricting the pleasures that might be constitutive of fineness. He then raises some further issues that cast doubt upon his definition. The line of thought he traces is this. Visual and auditory pleasures constitute the fine. A visual pleasure is pleasant in virtue of its visible and not (any) audible properties it might possess. An auditory pleasure is pleasant in virtue of its audible and not (any) visible properties it might possess. Therefore this definition fails the substitutivity condition because it's not true that something visually beautiful is beautiful because of its visual and auditory properties. *Mutatis mutandis*, audible pleasures. However, as Waterfield points out, this omits discussion of the disjunction of these two properties.[31]

Conclusion

The failure of the definitions in the *Hippias Major* has provoked scholars to look elsewhere for its true meaning. But this is predicated on the idea that Plato sought to conduct the sort of examination scholars hope to find in his work. At the very least, the dialogue reminds modern readers of the centrality of the fine in the work of the ancients and the possibility of a higher ethic.

CHAPTER SEVEN

Ion

Introduction

The *Ion* records a conversation between Socrates and Ion, a rhapsode, in which he tests his claim to expound truths about human life. It's frequently read in this connection as a precursor to, or trial run of, the later and more developed attack on poetry in the *Republic*.[1] The *Ion* is a very interesting dialogue and is distinctive in several respects.

First, while the other authentic dialogues are about ethics, the *Ion* is, ostensibly at least, about aesthetics.[2] Second, in the central section of the dialogue, Socrates departs from his characteristic method of asking questions to deliver two short and florid speeches about the origins of poetic inspiration. Third, the dialogue has proved stubbornly resistant to consensus. It has, for example, been both celebrated as a defence of poetry and denounced as a trivial attack on a thoughtless rhapsode.[3] In fact, scholars continue to dispute precisely what the dialogue is about: art; literary criticism; or even an early anticipation of Kant's distinction between fine and mechanical art.[4]

Although there is some general agreement about when Plato composed the *Ion*, sometime between 394 and 391, the dialogue's dramatic date continues to be controversial. This is perhaps not unsurprising given the very limited historical references it contains. A recent estimate, however, argues for a date between 406 and 402.[5] This would place the drama in the last few years before Socrates' trial, when hostility towards him was fermenting.

The drama

On the surface the drama of the *Ion* is relatively straightforward: Socrates accosts Ion, a successful rhapsode, and asks him whether his special ability is expressive of expertise. Rhapsodes were itinerant reciters of poetry who dramatised scenes from the poets and often lectured upon their meaning. A visit was a very significant event that captured the imagination of the local population, especially the young. Although Ion is often thought to emerge a bit of a fool from the dialogue, it is worth remembering that schoolchildren today flinch at the thought of memorising a sonnet. Ion had learned the whole of Homer's works off by heart.

When Ion confirms that he is an expert, Socrates presses him to state precisely what expertise he possesses. After some uncomfortable questioning he says it's the skill of generalship. However, in the closing moments of the dialogue, he retracts this claim and concedes instead that he is divinely inspired. Socrates only secures this concession by presenting Ion with a stark dilemma between his being unjust or divinely inspired. Ion's vanity explains his choice: he would always prefer to be favoured by the gods than to be thought unjust. The indecisiveness Ion displays throughout the dialogue suggested to Goethe that 'The Confounded Rhapsodist' would be a more fitting title.

But beneath the surface, matters of the greatest significance are at stake. Ion specialises in the exposition and interpretation of Homer's poetry (530a–b; 535d). The foundational role of Homer's works in Athenian society should not be underestimated. The *Iliad* and the *Odyssey* were common reference points for the whole community because they were believed to contain knowledge about almost every aspect of leading a successful, pious and honourable life (531c–d). If you wanted your son to develop an excellent character, for example, you encouraged, or compelled, him to memorise great chunks of Homer's poetry in the belief that he would thereby come to know what excellence was. To exaggerate a bit, the Homeric perspective became the shared perspective of the entire community: his poems unified and bound the society together. Shelley claimed that 'poets are the unacknowledged legislators of the world'. But it would seem, in this case, that they were in fact the acknowledged legislators of the world.

The rhapsodes thus rivalled the sophists as teachers of excellence and it's in this context that Socrates' interrogation of Ion should be examined. Ion thinks he's a custodian of the Homeric tradition: he believes he understands Homer's works and has taken it upon himself to teach others about the wisdom his poetry contains. Socrates, then, is challenging a very high-profile expositor of Homer to justify his activities with reference to his supposed expertise. Ion fails to do this convincingly. But the subtext of Socrates' argument is even more troubling. The poets themselves are vulnerable to the same arguments and this raises a question about the legitimacy of using Homer's poetry to educate people about human excellence. After all, if Homer's poetry does not contain knowledge about how best to live, then it loses its claim to be *the* authoritative source of instruction on the matter.

In appearing to attack Homer, Socrates was striking at the heart of the community, and it doesn't take much imagination to see that they would react rather badly to that. Among other things the *Ion* underscores why certain Athenians eventually found Socrates' quest for knowledge in ethics impertinent, offensive and perhaps even heretical.

Story and truth

Before we examine the *Ion* in any real detail it will be useful to first engage with its principal theme: story and truth. Why, it may be wondered, should we consider 'story and truth' and not 'poetry and truth'? Well, although Homer's a poet, both the *Iliad* and the *Odyssey* are narrative in form. Given this, and the contemporary popularity of stories over poetry, we will talk exclusively of stories as a matter of convenience.

Now, one of the ideas in the previous section that may strike the modern reader as a little weird is that of a community bound together by a set of stories. There's no comparable book in Western culture, for example, that must be read religiously by citizens who hope to succeed in life. Although the Bible may once have played such a role, it is popularly thought to play a less substantial role today (though it's not uncommon to find people citing Commandments as authoritative moral principles). But despite this, our faith in other stories and narratives seems unshaken: they continue to play as important a role in our community as the writings of scientists and philosophers.

There are, of course, conspicuous differences between stories and scientific or philosophical writing. Stories, for example, may try to please and to entertain, whereas much scientific or philosophical writing does not: few of us snuggle up in bed with cocoa and a copy of Kant. But for all the differences there is at least one interesting point of commonality: they all strive for truth. Now, the commitment to truth is conspicuous in the case of science and philosophy. Practitioners of both set out theses and theories in journals and books, the truth of which they hope to establish through argument and the citation of evidence. The same is certainly not (often) true of storytellers.[6] Their work is fiction and so comprises what is, on one level, a collection of falsehoods. So in precisely what sense do storytellers aim at truth?

We might begin by noting that for a number of storytellers striving for truth is part of their avowed aim. The likes of Italo Calvino, Harold Pinter and Peter Ackroyd have all said as much in articles or speeches.[7] Philosophers too have attributed this aim to literary writers: for example, John Stuart Mill and Iris Murdoch.[8] This list of luminaries may give us some confidence that we're not completely off beam in suggesting storytellers aim at truth. But it remains to be seen in what sense a story could be considered as presenting truths of life.

Consider the following example of popular storytelling on film. The romantic comedy *Groundhog Day* tells the story of a self-absorbed and acidic weatherman, Phil Connors, who finds himself trapped in a time-loop while on location in Punxsutawney. Phil's alternating reactions to his predicament are the source of many comical scenes in the film. He variously exploits and resents the seemingly endless repetition of February 2nd. But the film has subsequently become the focus of more serious study by theologians and philosophers because it captures a truth about humanity, something like: life is a prison until you learn to love something other than yourself. But how is such a truth communicated to the audience? None of the characters says anything like it in the film, nor do words to that effect appear before the credits as a kind of parting moral. One instructive way to think about this is in terms of metaphor. A story serves as a metaphor for life: where scientific and philosophical papers *state* the truth, stories *intimate* it. Their writers select actions and events from characters' lives and put them together in such a way that they hint at something universally true.

These sketchy reflections provoke some difficult questions of their own. We may, for example, worry about whether the truths stories allegedly intimate can be adequately distilled into pithy statements of the 'life is a prison ...' variety. We may also worry about storytellers' claims to know the truth. Does, for example, the truth of a story depend on its author's grasp of the truth? If it does, is 'being a writer' sufficient to discover it or is further empirical investigation required? Does the writer of a crime story, for example, have to acquire some of the expertise of a detective to write it competently? As we shall see, Socrates is particularly concerned with Ion's claim to speak the truth on the basis of expertise. The idea that storytellers do continues to be popular: Socrates' investigation, then, is as vital today as it was in ancient Athens.

The text

The question that drives the dialogue is whether Ion speaks about Homer on the basis of knowledge and expertise. The idea that writers possess such knowledge and expertise continues to command popular attention and presumably explains the appearance of writers in public debates on matters other than literature. When Ion confirms that he speaks about Homer with expertise (530c), Socrates sets out to test his claim by the application of the *elenchus*. There are three principal episodes in the dialogue:

- 531a–533c: in which Ion's claim to expertise is tested
- 533d–536d: in which Socrates outlines an explanation of poetic inspiration
- 536d–541b: in which Ion's claim to expertise is tested again

As we can see, the *elenchus* divides into two parts. In the first, 531a–533c, Socrates investigates the nature of Ion's ability and shows that it fails to exhibit an accepted characteristic of knowledge and expertise. However, even if that's true of Ion, it doesn't rule out the possibility that other rhapsodes, or even the poets themselves, *do* possess knowledge and expertise. In the second part, 536d–541b, Socrates develops an argument that would effectively rule out that possibility. He tries to show that any such poetic or rhapsodic expertise would not account for a person's knowledge of the subject matter of Homer. This amounts to an indirect attack on Ion's original claim to knowledge and expertise.

The two parts of the *elenchus* flank Socrates' own alternative explanation of Ion's ability: divine inspiration. The passage has been, and continues to be, remarkably influential. The success of the *elenchus*, however, does not hinge on the acceptance of this explanation. We will first examine both parts of the *elenchus* before turning our attention to Socrates' own explanation.

Finally, a note about translation. The terms '*techne*' and '*technai*' are of central importance to the *Ion*. Some translators use the same translation consistently so that the reader can be sure what Greek word Plato is using. Others try to reflect the various nuances of the word and so use 'art' to translate it in one context, but 'skill' or 'expertise' in another. The original Greek permits a broad range of translations including, for example, 'knowledge' on some occasions. For the sake of convenience and clarity we will, for the remainder of this chapter, use the English word 'expertise'.

531a–533c

The conclusion of the first argument of the dialogue is that Ion is an expert on Homer and on other poets as well (532b). Ion accepts the argument but believes the conclusion to be false: his expertise is limited to the works of Homer (532c). If Ion is correct and if the argument is valid, then at least one of its premises must be false. As we already know, Socrates proceeds on precisely this basis and suggests an alternative explanation for Ion's demonstrable ability. The pressing question, though, is whether Ion should accept Socrates' argument at all. In this section we will explore that issue by examining the cogency of an underlying assumption that Socrates makes.

Let's start by briefly considering the argument in full:

(1) Ion's expertise is rhapsody (530b–c)

(2) A rhapsode must understand the subject matter of the poetry he interprets for his audience (530c)

(3) Homer and the other poets address the same subject matter (531c–d)

(4) Expertises are wholes (532c–e)

∴

(5) Ion's expertise extends to the poetry of Homer and that of other poets (532b)

The most inscrutable premise in the argument is (4). Just what does it mean to say that an expertise is a whole? Take, for example, the expertise of carpentry. When we call a person an expert carpenter we mean he has a general and systematic ability with regard to the preparation and manipulation of wood for a wide range of purposes. If he can only work with pine and can only create simple lap joints, for example, he does not possess expertise in this sense. Ion claims he expounds the works of Homer with expertise. Since exposition requires the comprehension of a poet's subject matter (premise (2)) and the poets all have the same subject matter (premise (3)), he must be able to exposit the work of other poets as well.

Ion accepts the first three premises of the argument immediately. The fourth he accepts on the basis of the epagoge Socrates develops at 532e–533c. He argues from instances of systematic ability in the criticism of painting, sculpture, music and rhapsody to the universal conclusion that each expertise confers systematic ability across its entire domain. Ion freely admits that his ability is not systematic and is in fact limited to just one poet: the implication of this admission is that Ion's ability is not expressive of expertise (532c).

Commentators on this passage of the *Ion* have frequently concentrated on premise (4) and on the nature of expertise in general.[9] This is, of course, a very promising line of inquiry because if it turns out that expertise does not confer systematic ability in a given field then there is, on the face of it, nothing suspicious about Ion's apparently exclusive expertise about Homer. The results of this work have by and large confirmed Socrates' characterisation of expertise and have substantiated it with references to other

Platonic dialogues. We will not pursue that line of inquiry here. An alternative starting point, however, is premise (2), which expresses Socrates' analysis of the specific expertise he attributes to Ion.

The point of (2) is that, for a rhapsode to judge the excellence or otherwise of a particular passage of poetry, he must possess knowledge of what the passage is about. A carpenter, for example, won't know whether a layman has correctly described the procedure for producing a dovetail unless he knows what a dovetail is and how it's made. Socrates has suggested that Ion's expertise in Homer amounts to expertise in all the subjects Homer addresses. However, it is by no means clear that this is the correct way to portray Ion's expository power. To see this, consider the following alternative, which neither Socrates nor Ion mentions in the dialogue.

Christopher Janaway has suggested that poetic expertise might include understanding 'rules for writing or reciting in a set metre, knowing precisely what marks the difference, in the epic genre, between narration and a speech in character, perhaps even which modes of diction are appropriate for poetry as opposed to prose'.[10] Now if we were to characterise Ion's expertise in terms of knowledge of these formal elements of poetry, he could accept the conclusion (5). His knowledge of poetic form would apply equally to Homer and the other poets.

It doesn't matter, for our purposes, whether Ion would accept such a characterisation of his expertise. (As it happens he probably would not: explaining the formal elements of poetry is hardly a crowd-puller and is anyway more fitting for a lowly schoolteacher than a successful celebrity.) The real point is why we should accept Socrates' analysis of Ion's ability over a competing analysis, such as Janaway's. This in turn raises the matter of how we identify an expertise at all.

In general an expertise is manifested in a range of activity: for example, the preparation of wood and the formation of joints in carpentry and the identification of ailments and the devisement of remedies in medicine. For a given range of activity, expertise is exhibited in systematic competence in the performance of that range of activity. The question for us, then, is what exactly is it that rhapsodes do? What is their activity? They speak about poetry. There are, of course, many aspects of poetry. We have already considered two of them: their subject matter and their formal elements. But there is much more to poetry than just that: it is a source of pleasure and entertainment; and it expresses and arouses emotions. We have in fact already noted some of these features in the context of our discussion of stories above. The rhapsodes themselves conveyed much of the excitement of the literature they presented in their performances.

Socrates, recall, has restricted rhapsodic expertise to speaking knowledgably about the subject matter of poetry. But even modest reflection on the nature of poetry suggests that such a restriction is unwarranted. We could argue on this basis that Socrates doesn't really understand what poetry is: for there is more to a poem than its subject matter. Perhaps he doesn't. But if he does know what poetry is, we must explain why he wilfully restricts the discussion to poetry's subject matter.

One plausible suggestion is that not all aspects of poetry are equally interesting to Socrates. He portrays his quest as an attempt to prove the Oracle wrong by finding a person with wisdom (*Apology* 21c). One group of people reputed to possess such wisdom was the poets, and Homer chief amongst them. A poem may please its audience, it may correctly exhibit a certain metre, but Socrates is only interested in whether it constitutes wisdom about life and the world. It will be worth having a couple of examples in front of us before we proceed.

In the first line of the *Iliad* the muse sings of the anger of Achilles. This is the controlling theme of the entire poem. We live today in an angry world in which the significance of anger is seldom appreciated. But Homer shows how destructive and self-perpetuating this emotion can be. In this sense, it enshrines a central truth about humanity. To take one more example, from the first book of the *Iliad*, we find King Nestor attempting to establish a truce between Achilles and Agamemnon:

> Son of Pelus, venture not to contend with a prince
> Forcefully, for he never has a portion of things on a par with that of others,
> Even a prince who holds the staff and to whom Zeus has given glory.
> If you are stronger in force, being the son of a divine mother,
> Yet Agamemnon is the superior[11]

Here we see Nestor emphasising those relationships vital to the continued existence of society. The prince retains his authority, visible in his possession of the staff, despite Achilles' superior strength. In this passage, Homer underscores this truth about communities by the dramatic context in which Achilles' passion threatens to undermine it.

As we noted above, the Athenians thought Homer's poetry contained authoritative knowledge about such matters and thus Homer was required reading for ambitious young men. Socrates' examination of poetry reveals his interest in it as a competitor to science and philosophy. It is in its claims to knowledge and truth that Socrates is interested in poetry and not in its ability to please a crowd.

But Socrates has distorted what is going on here. The word '*techne*' possesses a broad extension and could be used to indicate a person's trade. When Ion first accepts Socrates' compliments about his ability, he may well have had his work as a professional reciter in mind. He now finds himself committed to arguing that his trade constitutes a body of systematic knowledge.

Poetry's pretensions to knowledge may warrant Socrates' restricted conception of it in the *Ion*, but none the less it seems Socrates has conflated two distinct issues here: the wisdom or truth a poem may contain and the wisdom of the poet or rhapsode. Ion may not possess knowledge of the subject matter of Homer's poetry, but it does not follow that there is no truth in Homer's works. We will return to this issue in our discussion of Socrates' account of poetic inspiration in below.

So far, then, we have examined the principal assumption in Socrates' attack on Ion. However, even if the argument is successful, it's limited to people like Ion who believe that they are experts but that their expertise is not general and systematic. What about the possibility of other rhapsodes who, unlike Ion, claim to possess expertise across all the whole field of poetry? Such individuals could quite happily accept conclusion (5). The intelligibility of claims to general and systematic rhapsodic expertise are directly confronted in the second part of the *elenchus* which we will consider now.

536d–541b

In the final part of the dialogue, Socrates reprises his examination of Ion's original claim to speak knowledgeably about Homer. In terms of the dialogue's drama, it is Ion's rejection of Socrates' explanation of his expository abilities that prompts the reprise. Having previously argued that Ion's ability fails to exhibit an accepted characteristic of expertise, Socrates now argues that rhapsodic expertise alone could not account for Ion's ability to exposit the subject matter of Homer. Notice this argument is wider in application: possession of rhapsodic expertise alone will not enable *anyone* to speak knowledgeably about the subject matter of poetry. And although Socrates doesn't make the point himself, the same argument applies, *mutatis mutandis*, to the poets and any so-called poetic expertise they may claim to possess.

It will be useful to begin by considering the argument. Socrates asks Ion which subjects in Homer he speaks well about. Ion replies, truthfully enough, all of them: to his mind there is no passage in Homer he could not expatiate upon. Socrates then invites Ion to recite some lines about driving a chariot and asks him whether a charioteer or a doctor would know best whether Homer speaks the truth in these lines (537c). Ion confirms both that the charioteer would know best and that he would know best on the basis of his expertise in chariot racing. From this Socrates wins Ion's assent to two claims:

(i) Each expertise contains knowledge of a particular activity (*ergon*) (537c)

(ii) Expertises are individuated on the basis of knowledge of different objects (537d)

The reason the charioteer is the best judge of the passage from Homer is that he possesses knowledge of the activity of driving a chariot (claim (i)). The reason the doctor is not the best judge of the passage from Homer is that he knows about medicine and not chariot racing (claim (ii)). On this basis Ion concedes that a charioteer would also be a better judge than a rhapsode of the same passage because the passage refers to the object of the charioteer's expertise and not the rhapsode's.

The general principle Socrates draws from this exchange is:

(6) What a person knows by means of one expertise he shall not know by another expertise (537c)

That is to say, for example, knowledge of carpentry will not confer knowledge of medicine. Socrates proceeds to develop a lengthy epagogic argument for (6) in the passage 538b–539e. Ion concedes in each case that the doctor, the fisherman and the prophet will be better judges than a rhapsode of passages in Homer that belong to their respective expertises. Implicit in this concession is the following:

(7) Rhapsody is an expertise distinct from medicine, fishing and prophecy

If we put (6) and (7) together we can infer:

(8) A person will not know about medicine, fishing and prophecy on the basis of rhapsodic expertise

Now, (8) is inconsistent with Ion's claim to be able to speak with expertise about *all* the subjects Homer addresses (540a). His possession of rhapsodic expertise does not amount to knowledge of medicine and fishing, say. But (8) is none the less consistent with the existence of a subject matter that is peculiar to the rhapsode's expertise. We have not yet ruled out, then, the possibility that there is at least something in Homer that the rhapsode is uniquely qualified to talk about. However, it is far from clear, to Socrates at least, what that might be. When asked to identify the exclusive subject matter of rhapsody, Ion suggests that it is about what people should say (540b). Socrates attacks this mercilessly in the subsequent discussion by focusing on what people might say in the capacity of a shepherd or a doctor (540c). However, Ion's response is reasonable enough and on the right track: he's able to draw an audience in, build tension and manipulate their emotions (535d–e). More importantly, Ion grasps the significance of human actions: he brings out of Homer's poetry the meaning of this or that event. This may not reduce to a set of technical expertises, such as medicine, but Ion owes his tremendous success to his ability to do this for large crowds.

The argument ends inconclusively: Socrates fails to establish that rhapsody doesn't have its own subject matter. However, the structure of the argument suggests that any subject matter it does have will be severely limited. It certainly won't include anything belonging to other well-defined expertises such as medicine, architecture, strategy, carpentry, engineering and so on. But what about matters of even greater importance in Homer: his comments about goodness, excellence and piety? These are, after all, the basis of his foundational role among the Athenians. Socrates doesn't even appear to consider them as possible candidates for the subject matter peculiar to Ion's expertise.

Having outlined the argument, we must now explore its underpinning assumption. Socrates' argument relies on premise (6), which rules out a rhapsode's knowing anything of medicine, fishing and prophecy. Premise (6) is derived from claim (ii), which states that expertises are individuated on the basis of knowledge of different objects. This amounts to the claim that expertises are discrete and there is no overlap between them. If there were, it would be possible for a rhapsode to know something about an expertise such as chariot-racing after all. Allan Bloom has argued that there's a problem with claim (ii): the problem is that it's false.[12]

Bloom presents the idea of the 'master art (*techne*)': an expertise that takes as (part of) its object the product of a subordinate expertise. Take, for example, the expertise of saddle making. A horse rider knows what a saddle is for and is in a position to tell the saddle maker what to do. Bloom's point is not that the rider is *also* a saddle maker (cf. Socrates' suggestion that Ion might also know something about generalship (540d)): it's that his expertise as a rider *includes* knowledge of the expertise of the saddle maker. It is his ability to ride that enables him to comment with precision about the characteristics of a good saddle, for example. If there are master arts, then it looks like expertises are not individuated on the basis of discrete bodies of knowledge. And if claim (ii) is false, then Socrates is no longer entitled to (6) upon which the force of his argument depends.

The problem for Socrates is the existence of an expertise that includes knowledge belonging to another expertise. In the context of the previous example, does the rider's expertise incorporate knowledge of the saddle maker's? It is true that both the rider and the saddle maker are concerned with the same object: the saddle. But does that amount to the rider's possession of the saddle maker's expertise? It does not: the rider knows about effective riding positions whereas the saddle maker knows about the shaping and stitching of leather. Knowledge of riding positions does not itself confer knowledge of shaping and stitching leather. The existence of master arts is not inconsistent with claim (ii) because, although both are concerned with the same object, they do not know the same thing about it. On this basis, Socrates is entitled to claim (ii) because a master art and a subordinate expertise are still discriminated on the basis of knowledge.

The conclusion of the Socratic *elenchus* in the *Ion* is that neither poetic nor rhapsodic expertise confers knowledge of any other expertise. And the implication of this is that poets and rhapsodes do not deserve the place they occupy in Athenian society on the basis of knowledge they possess as poets or as rhapsodes.

533d–536d

We already know that in the middle section of the dialogue Socrates delivers speeches that purport to explain Ion's celebrated ability in terms other than knowledge and expertise. Ion's rejection of conclusion (5) prompts him to ask Socrates to explain why he can only speak about Homer and not the other poets. Socrates' suggestion is that Ion is actually divinely inspired. The passage has been, and continues to be, highly, though controversially, influential as the following summary makes clear:

In his *Defence of Poetry*, Shelley developed Socrates' ideas about the divine origins of poetry and reproduced the image of the magnet attracting a series of links in a chain. More recently both Kenneth Dorter and Christopher Janaway read Socrates' speeches as proposing an account of beauty or poetic success that has its source in something other than knowledge and expertise. But the passage also has its detractors. Goethe thought that the introduction of the notion of divine inspiration mystified rather than clarified the creative process. And more recently Suzanne Stern-Gillet has urged that we should take Socrates' account only half seriously and pay more attention to his explicit sarcasm.

What Socrates actually says is quite straightforward: good poetry is the work of gods not humans (534e). He uses the image of the magnet to suggest a causal relationship between a god, a poet, a rhapsode and his audience. The picture certainly appeals to Ion's vanity, probably because it places him closer to the gods than his audience, and he declares that Socrates' speech has touched his soul (535a).

Since Socrates does not present an argument for his account of the origin of poetry and rhapsody, its strength must reside in its power to explain and illuminate the phenomenon. However, its explanatory force must be weighed against its plausibility.

Socrates connects his explanation with a number of putative facts, the most conspicuous of which is Ion's inability to expound poets other than Homer. But he also mentions other characteristics of the inspired state: its absorbency (534a; 535b–e); its inconstancy (534b); and its involuntariness (534c). Socrates' speech is supposed to account for these facts in the following way. In a state of inspiration the god possesses the poet and in so doing disables the poet's own cognitive power: hence the apparently absorbed state the poet finds himself in. The state of inspiration is initiated by the god and not the poet: hence the involuntariness and inconstancy of being inspired. Finally, the relationship between poet and god is linear and so does not permit possession by another god: hence Ion's specific relationship with Homer and not with poets possessed by other gods.

In terms of its explanatory power, Socrates' account seems fairly strong. The proposed causal relationship between gods and poets seems to account for a number of perplexing characteristics of poetic composition. But we must now consider its plausibility. In its present form we can see that some people today are unlikely to take it too seriously. We live in an age in which increasingly many people believe in the non-existence of gods. Such people may reject any explanation that relies in part on the activity of divine beings. However, merely believing in gods does not, by itself, dispel the implausibility of Socrates' account. We are impressed by poetry partly because it is the work of human beings who have achieved some insight into life and the world. But gods are, on some accounts at least, omniscient, which diminishes the achievement of presenting the truth. Furthermore, there is the matter of quite why the gods do this at all: to construe their behaviour as, for example, desirous of something conflicts with their perfect nature. And if the gods' intermittent possession of human beings is not goal directed, is not willed, it raises questions regarding what it is about human beings and gods that causes this occasional possession of the one by the other.

But perhaps we do not need to confront these immense difficulties head on. One response to them is to simply subtract the (problematic) supernatural element and thereby remain true to the spirit, if not the letter, of Socrates' explanation. If we eliminate reference to gods, what remains of Socrates' original account? It seems rather little. The residual claim is that the fine speaking of the poet originates in something outside his control. This isn't so much an explanation of poetic inspiration as a restatement of its mysterious nature. It may well be the case that there is nothing more to be said about literary inspiration than this. But it would be naïve to pretend that a secular version of Socrates' explanation elucidates the original phenomenon.

Finally, it's important to note the implication of Socrates' argument with the general tenor of his examination of Ion. Nothing he has said has ruled out the possibility that poetry may contain truth about life and the world. His explanation of divine inspiration would seem to guarantee the truth of poetry whenever it is composed under genuine conditions of inspiration. But the point is that in the act of composition the poet does not know whether he is speaking the truth. Any truth his work contains is the not product, at least on Socrates' account, of his exercise of his cognitive faculties. This further undermines any claim poets, or indeed rhapsodes, have to possessing knowledge about the world. Their status as informal educators is to that extent undermined.

Conclusion

The *Ion* raises important questions about stories as a source of knowledge about the world. Socrates' arguments have enduring significance for those who believe, as many of us do, that a literary education is of great developmental importance for human beings. He challenges us to specify the basis on which we entrust the souls of young and old to writers and their works. Ion fails to make a convincing case for his claims to knowledge, but our continuing respect for stories as a source of wisdom demands we find a better response to Socrates' questions.

CHAPTER EIGHT

Laches

Introduction

The *Laches* is a distinctive member of the Platonic corpus in several respects. First, the philosophical discussion regarding the nature of courage (*andreia*) accounts for a little over half the text. The first 11 pages are devoted to a discussion of education and, in particular, the merits of *hoplomachy*, the skill of fighting in armour. And although many shorter dialogues open with a dramatic exchange, this uncharacteristic division of material seems to merit an explanation. Precisely why would Plato include such a lengthy 'introduction' to a comparatively short discussion of courage? If the true purpose is assumed to be the discussion of courage, the so-called extended introduction merits explanation. The obvious response, of course, is that the first part of the text *is* of philosophical importance and this has resulted in 'philosophico-dramatic' interpretations, which incorporate dramatic detail into philosophical argument.[1]

The second distinctive aspect of the *Laches* is the significance of its philosophical content. To take just one example, commentators note that the final definition of bravery rejected in the *Laches* (195a) is the same as the definition endorsed in the *Protagoras* (360c–d). What sense can we make of this apparent disparity? Perhaps the inconsistency can be dissolved in some way or perhaps one dialogue was written with a view to correcting the other. Since we are, in this book, assessing the dialogues individually, we won't seek to resolve these broader matters of interpretation here. Readers interested in following up the relationship of the *Laches* to the rest of the Platonic corpus will find guidance in the notes to this chapter.

The dialogue is set at some point between 424 and 418. The first date can be established on the basis of the text itself: Laches explicitly refers to the battle of Delium, which took place in 424 (181b). For the latter date we have to go beyond the text to independent sources that state Laches was killed in the battle of Mantinea in 418.[2] Any further specificity is conjectural and speculative. The date of composition is not known, though Kahn argues the *Laches* is the first of a group of three dialogues (the others being the *Euthyphro* and the *Meno*) on the nature of definition.[3] However, even if we grant the contention, the uncertainty regarding the dating of those dialogues renders the connection of little use.

The drama

The story of the *Laches* can be stated succinctly: Lysimachus and Melesias, who feel they have squandered their lives, seek the advice of two successful generals, Laches and Nicias, about how they can ensure their sons do not succumb to the same fate (179b–e). Their sense of failure in life is readily comprehensible when Lysimachus reveals their ancestry. His father was Aristides the Just, who earned acclaim during the Persian Wars. Herodotus describes him as the 'best and most honourable man [then] in Athens'.[4] Melesias' father was Thucydides the elder, the most prominent and long-standing political opponent of Pericles. Long must these men have walked in their fathers' shadows.

The decision to approach Laches and Nicias about the benefits of *hoplomachy* is entirely reasonable.[5] They were, after all, high-profile military men who could be fairly reckoned to have some sense regarding the foundations of a successful career. We might be surprised about the enthusiasm for participation in the military, especially a decade into the war with Sparta. To date, the effect of the war on Athens had been devastating. In 430 the city was ravaged by typhoid fever, which ultimately killed about a quarter of the population, including Pericles in 429. The war effort itself had had notably mixed results: the battle at Delium, for example, claimed the lives of just under a thousand Athenians in 424.[6] However, Lysimachus and Melesias are principally interested in the instrumental value of *hoplomachy* because their ultimate ambition is for the boys to win fame and a good reputation (179d).[7]

The generals disagree about the merits of studying *hoplomachy*. Nicias judges it to be worthwhile because it makes a man fit, inculcates discipline, is tactically advantageous and makes its possessor courageous (181d–182d). Laches points out that the teachers of *hoplomachy* find no work among the foremost military force in the region, the Spartan army. Furthermore, the man who just gave the display, Stesilaus, made a clown of himself in actual combat. And far from making men courageous, practices of this sort make people take foolish risks because it gives them an inflated sense of their own capacity (182d–184c). The dispute over skill and courage is reprised later in the dialogue. At this point they turn to Socrates, who steers the conversation towards the attempt to identify the nature of courage. There are two outstanding points of the drama worthy of noting here.

First, although Lysimachus and Melesias privilege education as the route to success for their sons, this salutary judgement is undermined by their lack of appreciation of the difficulty of the educational enterprise. The only reason they have recourse to Socrates is because the generals disagree with one another. Had they agreed, Laches would not have had to ask for an umpire. So far as he's concerned, then, the *problem* of his son's future could, potentially at least, have been resolved in minutes. This is, I think, a very telling observation of Plato's. The desire for 'quick fixes' hasn't gone away and is apparent today on the self-help shelves of bookshops where success in life is promised in minutes.

Second, and perhaps more interestingly, is what we learn about the psychology of the generals. The most conspicuous irony of the dialogue is that two respected military leaders are presented as ignorant of the nature of courage. How embarrassing for these men of action, these dignitaries, to whom the population of Athens turn for advice, to be revealed as ignorant of one of the decisive ingredients of military success. What is truly remarkable, however, is their puerile and petty squabbling in the final stages of the discussion. Laches sarcastically mocks Nicias' failure to arrive at a defensible definition, while Nicias accuses Laches of caring only about not being the sole individual exposed as ignorant. The disintegration of their earlier composure is readily explicable in terms of the importance for them of honour. Such is its place in the order of their deliberations that the slightest affront is felt to be intolerable and to merit a response. They order their conduct with reference to reputation and honour. The dialogue exposes the danger that lies in locating one's honour in the expressions of esteem of others. Nicias and Laches find themselves at one another's mercy.

Courage

Not all the virtues of antiquity stand on a like footing today. Aristotelian magnificence, for example, which is expressed in very large scale public benefaction, is today construed as elitist and therefore invidious. Courage, though, remains a widely respected and admirable trait. It is interesting to ask why some virtues continue to command approbation, while others have fallen into disfavour. The natural explanation that suggests itself is that the importance of this or that virtue varies with the lifestyles of the people in a given community. Justice, wrote Hume, would be perfectly useless in a community in which nothing was scarce.[8] Aristotelian magnificence strikes some people as elitist because we do not think a person's moral praiseworthiness depends on his possession of great wealth.

It is not, however, immediately clear that we can explain the continued high standing of courage in this way. Its importance to Athenians is straightforward: the city's future depended on it decisively. Defeated states were burned to the ground, their property plundered and their people massacred or enslaved. Since Athens did not have a professional military, it relied for its security upon the prowess of its male citizens. But we are not the Athenians: Western states have professional armies, and conscription in recent decades has been relatively infrequent. The possession of courage by adult citizens is arguably not, then, so central a matter for us as it was for them.

But the line of thought traced in the previous paragraph surely misses the point. Human beings at all times and places are affected by fear. Perhaps surprisingly, given advances in medicine and greater stability in agriculture, contemporary sociologists argue that we are in the grip of a 'culture of fear'.[9] In 2009 the Mental Health Foundation published research indicating that people in the UK now feel more afraid than they did a decade ago and that the world has become a noticeably more frightening place.[10] It is a platitude that fear is a negative emotion; it is something we seek to avoid or to be delivered from. This bears out the truth of Montaigne's remark that 'the thing I fear most is fear'. Courageous people are admirable, in one respect, precisely because they appear to have achieved supremacy over that to which many of us remain victims. This looks like a more plausible explanation of our esteem for courageous people.

However, the connection between courage and fear is not entirely straightforward. Are the courageous afraid or not? On the one hand, if a person felt no fear when, say, charging the enemy we might hesitate to explain his action with reference to courage at all because he seems insensitive of the danger he is in. Similarly, we wouldn't credit a person with courage who leapt from rooftop to rooftop because he was high on the drug ecstasy. But on the other hand, we're tempted to describe the courageous as fearless. The debilitating behaviours associated with fear, such as cowering in the corner and closing one's eyes, are not typically manifest in courageous actions. A useful way to approach this puzzle is to consider the nature of fear itself.

When a person experiences fear he is present to himself as a victim. He is, in that experience, stripped of whatever delusions he may have been under as to his command over his world and he is painfully aware of himself as the patient of external causes he cannot control. This is what we fear in fear.[11] The brave person, however, reasserts his authority: he is present to himself as a source of agency in the world and in this respect we may distinguish him from a frightened person in whom agency is diminished or has disappeared altogether. This way of looking at matters suggests that a courageous person is sensitive to his proximity to danger, and so is not a maniac. What is distinctive is the retention of his capacity to act despite his recognition of the risks to which he is exposed.

But if we think of courage as simply the capacity to contain fear, to arrest its tendency to perpetuate itself, then there doesn't seem to be anything to rule out the possibility that courage can be expressed in what is deplorable. After all, a villain may expose himself to danger, may experience fear and may have the capacity to silence it in order to carry out his despicable acts. It was on this basis that Schopenhauer denied courage to be a virtue at all.[12] Nor does he stand alone: some philosophers in the last century were similarly taken with the idea.[13] Nevertheless this conception of courage seems to rest on a mistake. Courage is not simply the capacity to contain fear: it implicates a sense of what is just and right.[14]

Consider these examples. The first concerns a maritime disaster. One night in March 1987 the *Herald of Free Enterprise* capsized shortly after it left harbour. The event took 90 seconds and one can scarcely imagine the panic on board. One man, however, descended into the ship in the dark and spanned a corridor with his arms and legs, thus allowing tens of passengers to use his body as a ladder to freedom. Without them, they may have perished. The second example is that of a person walking across hot coals on a self-mastery course, or something of that nature. We can imagine both individuals were afraid and both appear to have contained their fear in order to act. However, there is, to my mind, a world of difference between them because the former is expressive of an individual's judgement of the importance of human life, the need to save lives, give hope in jeopardy and so on. And although the fire-walker may in one respect seem especially impressive – in his not being carried along by a sense of righteousness – his judgement to do it does not reflect that sense of defending what is just and right.

This is not to say, of course, that courage is not vulnerable to corruption. A righteous person can become someone who primarily loves to be a 'person in the right', where the matter at hand takes second place. But our assessment of the acts that follow from this state of mind can be fairly appraised in terms of our estimate of the value of a person who acts for that sort of reason. Outward appearances may not disclose an individual's motivation, but were we to know it may well make a difference.

So, to bring together a reasonably long discussion, we can note a few things. First, a courageous person may feel fear and, in any case, is certainly sensitive to his circumstances. But second, his active love of others, of what is right and fitting, is none the less given full expression in his actions.[15] Our individual experience of fear reveals to us what a striking achievement this amounts to.

The text

The philosophical discussion of the *Laches* comprises the philosophical examination of three definitions of courage. These are all ultimately abandoned and the dialogue ends in *aporia*. However, the structure of the discussion is, according to some commentators, supposed to intimate Plato's answer to Socrates' primary question about the nature of courage. Nicias thinks that courage is knowledge and Laches think it's endurance. They differ, then, in their identification of courage with, respectively, cognitive and non-cognitive features of the soul. Plato's point, on this interpretation, is that a successful definition of courage must reflect both its cognitive and non-cognitive elements.[16]

Before we go on to consider the material at the centre of such discussions it will be worthwhile to consider the target of Socrates' inquiry. So far in this chapter I have used the word 'courage' to denote the object under consideration. This is a translation of the Greek word '*andreia*'. The root of the Greek word is the stem '*andr-*', which refers to an adult male. Thus the primary meaning of '*andreia*' is manliness. The word was, however, susceptible to a broad range of application and so did not always have sexually specific connotations. It could simply mean 'having a good soul'. However, in the *Laches* the word appears to be stretched to the limit: a person can be *andreios* in the face of illness or poverty, in public life and in resisting carnal indulgence (191d–e).[17] It is, of course, a comic strain on everyday English to describe a person's resisting sexual desire as a display of courage. When considering the definitions the interlocutors offer in the *Laches* it is well worth considering just how well they might accommodate the full range of cases Socrates places before them.

187d–189d

The theme of the drama is education and the *Laches* is populated with poor learners. The conclusion of Socrates' discussion with Melesias, for example, is that he and Lysimachus should not base their decision on a show of hands, but upon knowledge of the right course to follow (184d–185a). But within a few pages

Lysimachus reveals that he and Melesias will do whatever the generals and Socrates *think* is best (189d). So much, one thinks, for the commitment to proceed on the basis of knowledge. In the present passage, Nicias draws Laches's attention to the typical character of conversations with Socrates: they will find themselves on trial, arguing for their respective ways of life. There are a couple of salient points to note about their attitude towards Socrates.

Nicias is prepared to subject himself to Socratic examination. He claims he does not find it annoying but feels he may actually profit from it. The cross-examination (Nicias uses a form of the word '*basanismus*', which literally means torture) makes one more careful in life (188b). On the face of it, then, Nicias is a model student: he volunteers himself for examination and recognises its value, despite being well aware of its unpleasant character. It's worth watching Nicias' behaviour in the rest of the discussion to witness the development of this posture of a willing student.

Laches expresses a comparable degree of enthusiasm for learning but with one important qualification. He will only accept instruction from an individual whose words are in tune with his deeds (188d). That is to say, Laches will not tolerate being deceived. It is important to note in this connection his predicament at 194a–b: he grasps what courage is but cannot put it into words. Although he says there he wishes to persevere, he ends up mocking Nicias and handing the entire matter over to Socrates (200a ff.). Readers interested in pursuing the drama of the dialogue should keep in mind the question of the impediments to learning for Nicias and Laches.

190d–192b

Socrates states that they should begin by considering the nature of courage and only then, reflecting on those activities, inculcate it in young men (190d; cf. 190c). This is an instance of Socrates asserting the priority of definitional knowledge (see p. 19).[18] Thus Socrates asks Laches to tell him what courage is. This is Laches's reply: 'If a man is prepared to stand in the ranks, face up to the enemy and not run away, you can be sure he's courageous' (190e).[19] This definition satisfies neither the substitutivity nor the explanatory conditions for Socratic definitions. In the first place, the expressions 'stands and faces enemy' and 'is courageous' are not substitutable *salva veritate*. In the second place, we cannot explain all instances of courage in terms of standing and facing the enemy.

Socrates captures these points with reference to several specific examples. He notes that the Scythians fight as much in retreat as they do in pursuit and that the Spartan infantry on one occasion broke ranks and adopted cavalry tactics.[20] Socrates assumes that Laches believes both the Scythians and the Spartans are courageous. If he does, he cannot consistently retain his conception of courage because their courage is not expressed in standing to face the enemy. We might, though, wonder whether Socrates has obtained this result honourably. He has exploited one possible, though far from the natural, interpretation of Laches's original answer. In his examples both the Scythians and the Spartans are fighting the enemy: neither, however, is *moving in the enemy's direction*.[21] But that is not what Laches had in mind: I doubt he would, for instance, count an evasive step backwards to avoid the strike of a sword as a central instance of 'running away'. So, Laches should not be so ready to conflate his definition with Socrates' examples, because he was thinking of people who seek to save themselves in retreat rather than those who move away from the enemy tactically.

As it happens, Socrates does not rest on this argument: he goes on to indicate the extraordinary scope of courage. It can be shown, he suggests, in war, at sea, in the face of poverty and illness, and in resistance to pain, fear, temptation and indulgence (191d–e). We have already noted that this strains English usage. What is remarkable, though, is Laches' immediate, and enthusiastic, assent to this list of acceptable applications (ibid.).[22] One way to make sense of this is in terms of the primary meaning of *andreia*: manliness.[23] Although no longer popular usage, we know more or less what someone means when they tell someone to be 'a man about it'. And they might say this with regards to enduring pain or resisting desire for the sake of what is noble. The philosophical issue here is whether this response to Socrates' list is desirable: courage emerges as knowing and doing what is admirable, which appears to be little more than leading a good life. Although Socrates' list may look in danger of turning what is typically thought to be a thick concept into a thin one, it's possible that Socrates continues to think of it as having a specific sense. To anticipate Nicias' suggestion a person who knows what should be feared, for example, will be suitably afraid of dishonour and so on.

191e–193d

Having been provided with an example of an adequate response to 'What is F?' (191e–192b), Laches produces his second definition of courage: endurance (*karteria*, literally heartiness). However, endurance is a normatively neutral quality: it can be displayed in the pursuit of both admirable and despicable ends. Laches has already acknowledged as much in his contention that a person who acts out of false confidence is not courageous (184d). Courage, however, is not normatively neutral: it is fine, noble and worthy of admiration. Socrates thus reformulates the definition as wise endurance (192d). However, in his examination of this definition, he ignores the character of endurance altogether and concentrates his efforts on the identification of the wisdom Laches has in mind. This is significant for two reasons.

First, some commentators emphasise Socrates' comment that courage may well turn out to be endurance (194a). So, although Laches is quick to abandon the reformulated second definition, Socrates' objection pertains only to the kind of wisdom that may be present in courage and not to the element of endurance. This chimes with those interpretations mentioned earlier that find a Platonic account of courage lurking in the wings of the *Laches*. Second, Socrates' concentration on the cognitive element of courage is consistent with his alleged intellectualism: the claim that a person's judgement that *x* is good is sufficient to motivate a desire for *x*.[24]

Socrates invites Laches to identify the species of wisdom (partially) constitutive of courage. Rather than present Laches with an open question, however, Socrates offers some examples of his own (192e–193c). In each case, Laches concedes that the presence of such wisdom in combination with endurance would not constitute courage. It is on this basis that he agrees they have failed to speak correctly about the matter (194a). In our assessment of the passage we need to pay close attention to the examples Socrates produces. They include: shrewdness with money; medicinal expertise; knowledge of military advantage; and the skills of horsemanship, slinging, archery and diving down a well (192e–193c).

Although these all enshrine practical knowledge of some kind or another, there is no reason to suppose that it is their practicality that makes it tempting for Laches to reject them. The point of the examples is that the wisdom in question does not, with endurance, confer courage because it reduces the agent's exposure to risk. A person who knows how to use a sling, for example, has less to fear than a person who does not know what he's doing. And if he has less to fear, he is less courageous. The same applies to the soldier who has accurately calculated his advantage over the enemy: when *he* attacks he knows he has a very good chance of emerging victorious. His enemy, apprised of the same knowledge, is courageous if he attacks because he is in great danger.[25]

Laches is prepared to concede two points at this stage. The first is that people who undertake these activities without the relevant expertise are more courageous than those with the relevant expertise. The second is that these people are foolish and not wise. It's not clear, however, that Laches is bound to make either concession. In the first case, although the person lacking expertise is in more danger when he uses a sling, it doesn't follow that he's more courageous. He could be using a sling in an effort to impress a woman he hopes to seduce.

In the second case, although it's true that the person does not possess the relevant expertise, it plainly doesn't follow that he is foolish. Suppose you don't know how to drive and you find yourself and your children amid a terrifying natural disaster. You're certainly ignorant of the skill of driving, but your attempt to do so to save your family's lives is not obviously foolhardy. This is the point that Nicias relies upon when he is questioned by Laches (195c–e), although he fails to clarify it sufficiently for Laches to appreciate.

Laches has been brought to despondency because of the appraisal of risk. He believes that a display of courage involves an obstacle that deflects one from the realisation of what would otherwise be one's purpose. That's quite true, but as we've seen it does not of itself compel the rejection of Laches's definition.

194c–197e

The arrival of Nicias in the philosophical discussion raises a couple of questions about the development of the drama. Socrates' invitation to him immediately follows his getting Laches to reaffirm his dedication to the project of identifying courage. One might, then, expect them to continue the search, rather than passing the baton to another party. Nicias' opening remark is also strange because he gives the impression he's been tutting and shaking his head throughout the exchange between Socrates and Laches (194c). But if that was the case, why didn't he intervene earlier to set them straight? Nicias, in fact, died because he hesitated and Plato may have wished to intimate that shortcoming. Thucydides reveals that the broken Athenian army was ready to leave Sicily when an eclipse of the moon prompted Nicias to order them to delay for another month.[26] The delay led to the Athenian defeat and the most horrifying torment and death for the captured soldiers.

Nicias defines courage as knowledge of what is fearful and what is encouraging in all situations (195a). He claims to have derived this from Socrates' view that we are good in so far as we are wise and bad in so far as we are ignorant (194d). While Socrates acknowledges his view, he doesn't indicate whether he believes Nicias' definition of courage follows from it. Instead he pits Laches against Nicias, which seems nothing more than an instance of stirring.

Laches doesn't understand Nicias' definition, although this may have something to do with the initial formulation, which is terse and open to interpretation. Laches simply carries over the conception of wisdom operative in his discussion with Socrates, which was, recall, technical expertise. Thus he points out that doctors know what medical conditions are frightening and farmers know what environmental conditions are hazardous for crops. But we would not, he claims, describe either of them as courageous on this account (195b).

Nicias, however, tries to clarify his position: a doctor may know what this condition is, how dangerous it is for the patient and so on; but he does not know whether it is better for this or that person to live or die (195c). This gives the misleading impression that doctors are wise because of the accuracy of their prognoses. They of all people know whether a person is likely to recover. Laches then conflates Nicias qualification with prophecy and descends into an abusive attack (195e). We have already commented on the falling out of the generals. Nicias thinks Laches is on the offensive because he has been humiliated by Socrates and now seeks to do the same to Nicias. But Laches' sudden transformation is more puzzling than that. The truth is that Laches perceives Nicias to be presenting a version of his definition of courage. What galls him is Nicias' condescension coupled with what looks like his adoption of precisely the same view.

Laches is, however, wrong. Nicias distinguishes what we might think of as knowledge of fact and knowledge of value.[27] Although one natural way to interpret knowledge of what is fearful is in terms of knowledge of what poses a threat (e.g. being able to tell a real weapon from a convincing replica), Nicias actually has in mind knowledge of what is right and proper in human life. The Spartans at Thermopylae knew they were outnumbered. However, they judged a shameful and futile attempt to escape more fearful than to die fighting for their law. An attempt to flee or surrender would disclose their prizing life at any cost.

Nicias' point seems right. Imagine a husband and wife walking home late after a night out. Suddenly, they're confronted by a gang brandishing knives and the wife is seized. The husband was walking close to a low fence, over which he could easily vault and run for safety. If the husband were to do this, however, he would be a coward: he would not be doing the right and proper thing. And although he might escape with his life, he would also escape with tremendous shame at having abandoned to a band of thugs the woman he ostensibly loved. That, for Nicias, is the truly fearful prospect. The question, however, is whether this conception of courage bears scrutiny.

196d–199e

Socrates examines Nicias' definition in two ways: by pointing out an apparently unpalatable implication of the view; and by arguing that Nicias cannot discriminate between courage and the whole of goodness. He pursues the second line of attack at greater length, but the former is perhaps more puzzling to the modern reader. Socrates points out that Nicias' view implies animals and children, who are not *ex hypothesi* wise, cannot be courageous. The text suggests that Athenians were happy to describe animal behaviour as courageous. But today we may well be sceptical about whether an animal could possess virtue in anything other than an anthropomorphic sense. Although a lioness will react aggressively to what she perceives to be predators trying to abduct a cub, she is not doing so on the basis of a judgement about what is right. Nicias defends himself by distinguishing fearlessness from courage: only the former quality is present in the lioness. What's interesting, however, is that Socrates himself is committed to this view. He thinks courage is good (190d) and that the good are wise (194d). Thus, if he follows the conventional wisdom, which Laches endorses, he too will face the same dilemma. Either these animals possess wisdom or they cannot be courageous.

Socrates' final argument reprises the interlocutors' earlier commitment to the claim that courage is a part of goodness (190c). However, Nicias agrees that the fearful is future evil. If we presume that evil is one thing, then knowledge of future evil implies knowledge of evil simpliciter. But then the knowledge constitutive of courage is knowledge of the entirety of good and evil.[28] Although Socrates seems to reject Nicias' definition on these grounds, some commentators treat this passage as an argument for the unity of the virtues. Courage is, on this account, virtue itself (*mutatis mutandis* justice, piety and temperance).

The first point to note is that Socrates' earlier list of cases in which courage may be displayed is rendered comprehensible under his reading of Nicias' definition. How are we to understand courage in the face of sensual temptation? Presumably not in terms of the potential sensory gratification itself which, *qua* pleasure, is pleasant and attractive. What is to be feared is the commission of something shameful, degrading and wrong. A courageous person, then, must be apprised of knowledge of good and evil on Socrates' account too.

The second point is that Nicias has committed himself to a form of intellectualism. Socrates does not investigate this here: he is more concerned about whether Nicias has isolated courage from the other virtues. However, we may profitably explore the underlying assumption. Nicias thinks the difference between a courageous person and a coward consists in the former's knowledge of the fearful and the latter's ignorance. What, though, are we to say about cases in which a person does not intervene in a situation he knows to be wrong? He may be full of self-chastisement, cursing his own weakness. Can we simply explain all this in terms of an absence of knowledge? The person in question may judge that what is happening is wrong, but he also judges he doesn't want to incur injury because he intervenes. He privileges the avoidance of injury over the prevention of wrongdoing. It is with respect to this judgement that, on the intellectualist model, he makes a mistake.

Conclusion

There are a couple of striking points to take away from the *Laches*. The first is the ease with which a fascination with honour breeds feuds, even between good friends. The second is the implied discrimination of a non-technical species of knowledge in courage. The dialogue sets the stage for a deeper discussion of courage such as the one we find in Aristotle's *Nicomachean Ethics* (III).

CHAPTER NINE

Meno

Introduction

The *Meno* remains one of the most popular shorter dialogues. It is renowned for the claim, apparently defended by Socrates, that knowledge is *a priori* and that education is a species of recollection. However, the dialogue covers many more issues than that. Perhaps the most striking, if neglected, claim is that virtue originates in divine dispensation (99c). This is, in one sense, a particularly unattractive view because, for philosophers who restrict responsibility to voluntary action, it implies that being virtuous or vicious is apparently something we cannot do anything about. However, I will suggest below that Socrates took this idea seriously.[1]

The *Meno* is conventionally treated, by commentators wedded to developmental readings, as a transitional dialogue. The first part shares commonalities with so-called early dialogues because of the posing of 'What is F?' and the rejection of answers to it. But the middle and final sections are thought to incorporate Platonic elements, such as the Forms, which the slave boy grasps at some time before his birth.

The dialogue is set after the restoration in 403 and before Meno's ill-fated departure into the heart of Persia in 401. As will become clear when we consider the story of the *Meno* the appearance of Anytus, generally thought to be the driving force behind Socrates' prosecution, may suggest it closer to 401 than 403. The date of composition is not known, but the explicit use of Pythagorean geometry suggests it was written after Plato's first visit to Sicily in 387 (which was where he is thought to have first encountered these ideas).

The drama

When Socrates asks the sophist Gorgias whether oratory can be taught to a student who does not know good and bad, right and wrong, he replies: 'I suppose, Socrates, that I shall have to teach a pupil those things as well, if he happens not to know them' (*Gorgias* 459d–460a; cf. *Meno* 95c). Gorgias thus confirms both that these matters can be taught and that he possesses the capacity to teach them. The young and wealthy Meno, however, is not so sure: he is in two minds about the issue; sometimes he thinks it can be taught, other times not (95c). So, he has approached Socrates with a view to his settling the question.[2] The question itself, whether virtue can be taught, was a popular and enduring one. It is, for example, central to the *Protagoras*, which is set some 30 years earlier. What is interesting in the *Meno* is not that it is asked, but that it is asked by someone like Meno.

Meno later achieved notoriety for his involvement in an effort to overthrow the King of Persia in 401. That sorry tale originates in nothing other than a case of sibling rivalry. After the death of Darius II of Persia his elder son, Artaxerxes, came to the throne. A deception was practised upon Artaxerxes to the effect that his younger brother Cyrus was plotting against him. He had Cyrus arrested and was going to put him to death. Cyrus escaped, gathered an army and began what would become known as the march of the ten thousand. Meno was one of Cyrus' generals. The mission failed; Cyrus and the other generals were executed.

Xenophon characterises Meno as a greedy, duplicitous traitor. He claims that, unlike Artaxerxes' attitude towards the other conspirators, he was so disgusted with Meno he held him in torment for a year before being executed. The truth of this is questionable: Xenophon was loyal to Meno's rival, Clearchus.[3] None the less, Joseph Klein points out that Plato's readers would have been aware of Meno's reputation for vice and that he may have exploited this for ironic effect.[4]

However, Meno's betrayal of his fellow Greeks occurs after his conversation with Socrates.[5] He is not yet the vicious character Xenophon makes him out to be. We have, then, at the very least the suggestion that their discussion did not prevent the development of his later vicious character and the hint that Socrates may actually have contributed to it. But we are yet to ascertain why Meno, with his alleged underlying greed, should care so much about the acquisition of virtue. It's at this point that we should remind ourselves of the popular usage of the term '*arete*' (translated here as virtue). If we treat this is an exclusively moral term, we get the impression that the Athenians were anxiously competing to be the most morally upright of people and were even willing to compensate teachers of morality financially. But the Athenians actually sought to be successful and the possession of the *aretai* was popularly thought to deliver this. In one respect, the Athenians pursued the virtues as we pursue social and leadership skills in business. According to popular belief, if you have those, you'll make a lot of money.

Meno is, then, an ambitious young man. He is familiar with the terms of the debate about the origin of virtue and he turns to Socrates for advice on the answer. The dialogue concludes with Socrates expressing scepticism about the possibility of a person's acquiring virtue through teaching (98aff.). 'Whoever has [virtue] gets it by divine dispensation without understanding' (99e).

Meno does not emerge from this dialogue as an obviously vicious young man. Plato does, however, portray him as a poor, and a lazy, learner. He's reluctant to apply himself to the conversation in hand and relies on what he has heard others say (see, e.g. 71e; 76c; 80d). We all, no doubt, share in this fault some of the time. Schopenhauer, commenting upon our tendency to read passively, wrote that 'reading is merely a surrogate for thinking for yourself; it means letting someone else direct your thoughts'.[6] So perhaps even in this respect we can see ourselves as having something in common with the youthful Meno.

Can virtue be taught?

In the previous section we noted that the Athenians did not conceive of the virtues as what we might nowadays call moral qualities but as the traits of the best and most admirable people. However, it is worth starting by considering whether moral qualities, such as conscientiousness, can be taught. That is how we tend to first appreciate the question and is particularly interesting because ordinarily people do seem to think that morality can be taught. This is most conspicuous when young people fail to behave in the way those in authority would like. In the UK, for example, parents of children persistently committing minor offences can be subject to a Parenting Order. This is a legal mechanism by which parents can be held responsible for the actions of their children. The clear implication of this is that parents are capable of developing some minimal sense of law-abiding conduct in their children.

But any such *belief* about the power of parents to teach their children to be good does not imply that it is actually possible. But before we can consider this, we need to have some sense of what it is to learn to be good. If we reflect on what people tend to have in mind by moral education, it boils down to being told this or that is right or wrong. After having been informed of this, transgressions are subject to sanctions. In other times and places, the character of these sanctions was typically physically coercive: children would be smacked or given a 'good clip round the ear'.[7] Corporal chastisement of this character is, nowadays, looked down on by some and a parent may only smack his child as 'reasonable chastisement'. Sanctions now include the 'naughty step' or 'time-out zones' in which children are removed from a situation and given time to reflect. The question we need to consider, however, is whether this is teaching morality. Have children who are responsive to this learned to be moral?

The children exposed to this pattern of adult conduct may associate actions of a certain sort with the linguistic habits of their parents. 'When I do this, Mummy says it's wrong and makes me sit over there and then come and say sorry.' But even if such a pattern is impressed upon the child, it's far from clear that he has grasped what is *wrong* about his behaviour. If the child continues to be tempted to behave in that way, and if he doesn't like hearing his mother say it's wrong etc., he learns not to do it when she's around. But the acquisition of the epithet 'wrong' does not automatically render the behaviour repulsive to him in the way it is to his mother. No doubt this is not what is realistically intended anyway: what we want is to establish a pattern of behaviour in such a way that it becomes 'second nature'. However, as we have noted, it's not clear that these practices, by themselves, even deliver that more modest result with any reliability.

So, what about the more ambitious goal of teaching people to recognise what is wrong in conventionally frowned-upon behaviour? One approach is to try to help the child appreciate the significance of his actions. Rousseau recommended something like this in *Emile*, his book on education:

> I have said enough to make it understood that punishment as punishment should never be inflicted on children, but it should always happen as a natural consequence of their bad actions. Thus you will not declaim against lying ... but you will arrange it so that all the bad effects of lying ... come in league against them when they have lied.[8]

There is a sense here in which the parent, through his conduct, is developing in the child some grasp of the wrongness of lying. But it remains true that for this strategy to work the child must be sensitive to the badness of the bad effects of lying. We can readily imagine a depressed and miserable child, to whom the world is ugly and depressing, remaining insensitive to these effects. What to him is the marginal significance of not being believed in this otherwise miserable state of affairs in which he lives? He has first to be moved to love and cherish aspects of his world for the contrast Rousseau is suggesting to be appreciated.[9]

But even if we suppose the presence of a positive attitude and a desire for success in life, it's not obvious that this focuses the learner on the good and the evil of moral actions. In the *Protagoras*, for example, the young Hippocrates is *desperate* to become the sophist's pupil. He hopes Socrates has the sophist's ear and can pave the way for his becoming Protagoras' student. While it is quite true he has a desire for something, it's not obviously the case that it is a desire appropriate to learning. Think of the incentives used today to encourage young people into Higher Education. A degree will improve your job prospects, which are vital if you want money, which in turn is vital if you want your own place, access to the internet and TV. The effect of this is to encourage students to ask whether this or that is going to be part of the exam. And they're quite right: if it's true that the value of education lies in the acquisition of a degree, then their efforts should be tailored to the terms of that task.

The acquisition of goodness, then, would seem to depend on a combination of factors. The difference between the good and the bad is not simply the fortune of the former to have been exposed to the right teacher.

The text

Scholars traditionally divide the *Meno* into two lengthy sections: 70a–79e and 80a–100b. The second section is then further subdivided.[10] As we have already noted in the introduction, developmentalists treat the *Meno* as a transitional dialogue falling between Plato's early and middle periods. The first section of the dialogue is thought to be predominantly Socratic and the second section predominantly Platonic. Thus we find Socrates posing 'What is F?' and the elenctic scrutiny of Meno's definitions of virtue in the first section. In the second, Socrates speaks of the Forms as the objects of knowledge, which Plato would later develop in, for example, the *Phaedo* and the *Republic*. There is no suggestion, however, that the *Meno* has been welded together like the serviceable parts of a couple of stolen cars. Commentators think Plato is answering in the *Meno* the (historically) Socratic mode of philosophising, 'stepping out from behind his lead character Socrates' and doing philosophy his way.[11]

Owing to the length of the *Meno* the comments in this section will be selective, but I hope those selected will prove to be useful. I have included references in the notes for readers wishing to concentrate on particular themes in the dialogue, but I have tried to give due weight to each part of the text.

70a–71d

Meno seeks an explanation for a person's possession of virtue. He presents Socrates with a list of alternatives to choose between: teaching, practice, native inheritance or something else (70a). This was a popular issue of the day in intellectual circles. The sophists, for example, advertised themselves as teachers of virtue. But, as Socrates points out in the *Protagoras* (319e–320b), virtuous people themselves often fail to impart it to their offspring. If we assume charitably that these people at least attempted to do so, we face questions about whether the acquisition of virtue can be accounted for in terms of teaching.

What makes Meno's asking this question puzzling, however, is his sense of the nature of virtue. He initially defines the virtue of a man in terms of his governing the state in such a way as to benefit friends and harm his enemies (71e; 73d) and later as the capacity to acquire gold, silver, high office and honours (78c–d). If that's what Meno thinks manly virtue amounts to, we might wonder why he thinks the explanation of it is so very problematic. He's really interested in manipulating and persuading people: we accumulate wealth by persuading people of the value of things in our possession and we achieve positions of governance through persuading people we know what's in their interests and how to achieve it. Presumably this owes to a combination of natural endowment, practice and circumstance. But the power of persuasion, of charming people, seems a relatively modest ambition compared with the achievement of human excellence.[12]

However, it must be admitted that even Meno's more modest ambition appears to hang defiantly out of reach. There are countless courses and consultants working today to impart these skills to people and there is no guarantee that patient submission to instruction will make one better able to persuade others. Furthermore, Meno himself is not willing to make an effort to work things out for himself: he wants to be told. So even if he appreciates the difficulty, he wants a ready answer and a world tailored to his desires.

Socrates ducks the question and flatters Meno's native Thessaly instead. He surprises Meno by claiming that no one in Athens even knows what virtue is, never mind their knowing how to produce virtue in others (71aff.). This provides a pretext for the insinuation of the principal theme of the dialogue. Meno asks Socrates whether he heard Gorgias speak when he visited the city and did not learn from him. Socrates characteristically says he can't remember. Learning, memory and recollection are, as we shall see, the recurring themes of dialogue (see, e.g. 71d; 73c).

71d–79e

Socrates begins by explicitly asserting the priority of definitional knowledge (see p. 19) and thus argues that he and Meno must first state what virtue is before judging whether or not it can be taught (71c–d). Meno provides three answers to this question: the first is at 71e, the second 73c and the third 77b. All three are abandoned in the face of typical Socratic questioning. Before we consider his answers, however, we should note a worry about whether Socrates really seeks an answer to his 'What is F?' question. This raises important questions about Socratic definitions and so it will be useful to start with this issue and then appraise Meno's definitions in light of it.

In Chapter Two we noted that 'What is F?' invites a real definition, a specification, that is, of the essence of F. In some shorter dialogues, Socrates offers model answers to 'What is F?' to help his interlocutors along (e.g. quickness is doing a lot in a short time (*Laches* 192a–b)). He does this in the *Meno* too (73e–76d). The problem is, Socrates' answers are not all of a piece.[13] He draws his examples here from geometry: two of shape and one of colour. Socrates first defines shape as the only thing that always accompanies colour (75b) and then as the boundary of a solid (76a). He defines colour as an effluence commensurable with sight and perceptible by it (76d). The first definition of shape does not specify its essence: it merely identifies shape without telling us what it is. The second definition of shape looks like an analytical statement: the boundary or limits of a thing are what we mean when we speak of its shape. The definition of colour does specify a real essence. Crombie notes that 'it seems fair comment that the models Socrates offers suggest he is not too clear he wants an answer to a Socratic question'.[14]

There are various responses to this interpretative problem. David Charles, for example, argues that these are not confused answers to one question, but precise answers to two questions.[15] The first question is 'What is F?' and the second is 'What do you call by the name "p"?'. This second question can be adequately answered in terms of an identifying statement, such as shape is what always accompanies colour, or an analytical statement, such as shape is the boundary of a solid. If we accept this reading, we do not need to saddle Socrates with a confused conception of an adequate answer to 'What is F?'. Charles notes, however, several grounds for being pessimistic with regard to Socrates' awareness of such a distinction – in particular, his claim that he would be satisfied with a definition of virtue modelled on his first definition of shape (75b), which does not specify an essence. However, it is not clear that we have to resort to these more or less curly explanations.

It's clear that Meno appreciates the possibility of the multiple instantiation of a single property. He is happy to admit that strength, for example, is one thing and that it may be present in a man or a woman (72e). What he hesitates to accept is that there is a single property instantiated in all the individual virtues: courage, piety, justice and temperance. Socrates aims to tackle this by presenting Meno with a case of a square and a circle. These exhibit significant differences but are none the less both shapes. In this respect they contrast with the case of strength that is the same in all instances. Socrates is, then, trying to help Meno appreciate this point, which is the obstacle preventing him from participating competently in the discussion.

We turn now to the definitions Meno offers. Socrates does not treat them at great length and it's tempting to think we don't learn very much about the character of virtue from the passage and that Plato's principle purpose is to consider the nature of Socratic definitions.[16] However, Meno's definitions disclose much about popular ways of thinking about virtue.

Meno's first response to Socrates' question comprises two parts. In the first he enumerates the virtues of men (running the state), women (managing the household), male and female children, older men and slaves. In the second he makes a more general claim about the range of virtues: 'for every act and every time of life, with reference to each separate function, there is a virtue for each one of us, and similarly, I should say, a vice' (72a). This looks like, and is treated as, a misunderstanding of Socrates' question. But it is importantly different from, say, Laches's first response to 'What is F?' (see p. 122). In the first place, Meno has referred to a plurality of virtues as opposed to providing a narrow definition of one. In the second place, Meno has stated that virtue is (in some unspecified way) related to functions (*erga*). Although this does not amount to an adequate definition of virtue, it does intimate to us something quite general about virtue itself.

Socrates ignores the second part of Meno's answer altogether and concentrates his response on Meno's failure to specify the common form (*eidos*) running through the virtues (72d). It's worth noting, though, that in the *Republic* Socrates himself characterises the virtue in terms of properties that enable a given thing to carry out its function well (352d–354b). Aristotle too made effective use of the notion in the *Nicomachean Ethics* (I.7). So, although Meno has not stated what makes this or that an instance of virtue, we should not rush to dismiss his first response as egregious. We can, however, already see a fundamental division between the way the two speakers think about virtue.

Meno conceives of the virtues as discrete and heterogeneous properties.[17] We can explain this in terms of his concentrating on the surface: he looks at the visible behaviour of virtuous people. If one conflates virtues with virtuous actions, then one may be tempted to think of them in terms of discrete activities. A virtuous woman, for example, is careful with household goods and obeys her husband. If you see a woman behaving like that, you can be sure she's virtuous. But Socrates conceives of the virtues as having some common form that they all share. This commonality of form justifies our referring to them as virtues in the first place. It is remarkable that Socrates doesn't draw more attention to this difference between them. Although in the present passage (73b), and later when criticising Meno's claim that acquiring silver and gold is virtue (78d), Socrates mentions doing so justly and temperately, he does not point out that this goes deeper than the surface of behaviour. Since Meno's failure to appreciate or accept this way of thinking is decisive to their shared failure to make progress, it is puzzling why Socrates doesn't address the matter explicitly.

Meno's second response is that virtue is the ability to govern mankind. While this chimes with Meno's earlier conception of the virtue of a man, it is conspicuously inconsistent with the virtue of a slave, as Socrates immediately points out. It would seem that Socrates must bear some of the responsibility for Meno's failure here. When commenting on what Meno has said, he states that they have failed to find the single virtue that permeates them all (74a). This is a puzzling way of making the point. After all, it sounds a little odd to claim that the virtues possess a virtue. It rather gives the impression that Socrates wants the name of a virtue in addition to courage, temperance, wisdom and justice that is present in all the others. This is the task with respect to which Meno professes himself to be at a loss: he can't name another virtue that the individual virtues all share.

Socrates tries to address the problem by considering the case of shape, which we considered above. In the aftermath of that demonstration, Socrates invites Meno to state the nature of virtue and this results in Meno's production of his final response. Virtue is the desire for, and ability to obtain, fine things (77b). Meno has forgotten his earlier concession that for a man's governance of the city to be virtuous it must be just.[18] He has not, then, learned from Socrates' examples.

Socrates begins by disqualifying the reference to a desire for fine things because that is, he argues, common to all people. This enshrines Socrates' intellectualism and is referred to as the first Socratic paradox.[19] This is said to be a paradox because it conflicts with our intuitions: we ordinarily take people to be capable of forming desires that are independent of their assessments of what is good and what is not. These non-rational desires are necessary for the possibility of *akrasia* (acting contrary to our judgement of what is best). Socrates, however, denies that anyone desires something bad as a bad thing that he believes will cause him harm (77e). We will consider the issue further in our discussion of the *Protagoras*.

80a–86c

We now turn to the most famous passage of the dialogue: Meno's paradox and Socrates' examination of the slave. These have received considerable attention in the literature and we shall limit our comments here to one or two broad features of the episode: the relationship between the paradox and the account of learning as recollection; and the two conceptions of learning.

Socrates suggests that they return to the start of their inquiry and Meno responds by accusing him of witchcraft: he is like a torpedo ray, which numbs its victim (80a). Socrates denies the comparison and reasserts his earlier denial of knowledge about the nature of virtue. It is in response to this that Meno articulates his paradox: how can Socrates search for something if he doesn't know what it is (81d)? It has been suggested by some commentators that this is a mere tactical move on Meno's part.[20] The plausibility of that suggestion is confirmed by the fact that Meno could have raised the same problem at the beginning of their discussion (71d).

He has subsequently been shown to be ignorant and so now fights back using his eristic argument.[21] However, his paradox raises a substantial problem and one that calls for a sensitive response.[22] Meno states his puzzle thus:

> How will you look for something when you don't know in the least what it is? To put it another way, even if you come up against it, how will you know that what you've found is the thing you didn't know? (80d)

There are two points here: (i) we cannot look for something if we don't know what we're looking for; and (ii) if we don't know what we're looking for we cannot know when we've found it.[23] Contemporary scholars dispute the precise meaning of the paradox, but the threat Socrates perceives it to pose is quite clear: 'we ought not to be led astray by the contentious argument you quoted. It would make us lazy and is music to the ears of weaklings' (81d).[24] If we can neither conduct nor confirm the success of our inquiries, we shouldn't bother undertaking them. This chimes with Meno's broader conception of learning, to which we shall return below.

In response to Meno's paradox Socrates claims that learning is a matter of recollection: the soul is immortal and acquired its knowledge in the other world; in this world the soul forgets what it has known before and what is called learning is an act of recall (81c–e). This famous passage has spawned a large literature of its own. We shall, however, sidestep the body of that and concentrate on one central issue: whether the account of learning as recollection constitutes a response, plausible or otherwise, to Meno's paradox. If it fails in this regard, it doesn't matter whether or not the more minor points of the discussion can be made out.

The problem Meno has posed is whether inquiry is possible; the account of learning as recollection is an explanation of how we know about the world. Suppose it's true that if we know that *p* we have recollected that *p* from a time before we were in human shape. But this doesn't obviously solve the paradox of inquiry because either we have recollected *p* or we have not. If we have, we cannot inquire after *p*; if we have not, how will we go about recollecting *p* having no idea what it is we're hoping to recollect?[25] However, we can attenuate this worry in the following way. Socrates could contest Meno's assumption that we do not know 'in the least' what we're looking for: we may well have some sort of specification or desiderata for our inquiry. A lonely heart, for example, may seek someone tall, dark and handsome without knowing it was Frank he wanted after all.[26] This, then, raises the question of the precise business of the account of learning as recollection. We now return to Meno's conception of learning.

Through the text Meno has treated learning as a matter of being told something by someone else (e.g. 75a–b; 76a). He likes to be told things and even suggests his willingness to stay in Athens if Socrates produced more definitions like his one on colour (77a). Learning for Meno is a passive matter: the world impresses itself upon the soul and leaves its mark. Socrates opposes this account and the example with the slave is supposed to loosen his commitment to his conception of learning.

Socrates sketches a four-foot square and asks the slave to specify the length of the side of an eight-foot square (82e). The slave provides two wrong answers and then, after a period of perplexity, produces the correct answer. Since Meno confirms that nobody taught the slave the answers, Socrates suggests that he must have known them already (85d–e). On this account, what we 'learn' is already in us and is acquired through effort (85c). Although much is made of Socrates' sophistic use of leading questions[27] to produce this minor miracle before the genuinely astonished Meno, he concludes the episode by retracting almost all of the details (86b).[28] The point he has made, and which Meno has accepted, is that it is right, proper and brave to inquire into what one doesn't know.

At the core of the case, then, is the distinction between an active and a passive model of learning. The distinction survives today in what is called teacher-centred and student-centred learning (with a preference among professionals for the latter). Meno prefers the teacher-centred model and Socrates the student-centred. Although the distinction can really only be maintained through exaggeration (successful students of the teacher-centred approach are not fairly described as passive), we can see that learning involves the active connection between ideas in the minds of students. In this book, for example, I have described the 'problem of the *elenchus*'. Learning what this problem amounts to involves more than being exposed to, or remembering, the propositions 'Socrates brings together inconsistent propositions' and 'Socrates declares one proposition false on the basis of the inconsistency'. To learn what the problem is, one must recognise that an inconsistency between propositions does not, by itself, imply the falsity of one or the other. The learner must make an effort to combine these ideas until they 'click'.

We have skated quickly over this passage but we can see that it succeeds in what I have suggested is its primary purpose: to disabuse Meno of his argument that defends his lazy approach to learning. Readers wishing to explore the details of the slave example are recommended to consult Scott (2006) for a recent, thorough appraisal of the argument.

86c–100b

Having agreed that inquiry is possible and proper, Socrates poses his 'What is F?' question again. Much to his exasperation, Meno replies that he would prefer to pursue his question about whether virtue can be taught (86d). After venting his frustration, Socrates agrees and proposes that they proceed on the basis of hypothesis. Despite their not having ascertained the character of virtue, they can consider what kind of a thing virtue would have to be in order to be transmitted through teaching.

Socrates states that virtue could only be taught if it is a kind of knowledge (87b). The question, then, is whether or not virtue is knowledge. It may appear that Socrates has cunningly returned to 'What is virtue?' and not 'Is virtue teachable?'. After all, he is committed to the priority of definitional knowledge. They are now embarked once more on the investigation of a claim about the character of virtue (despite Meno's not having noticed). However, the results of a hypothetical inquiry are conditional: for example, virtue is knowledge (on the condition that virtue can be taught). This is not equivalent to knowledge of virtue, which is (under some interpretations) the goal of the *elenchus*.

The passage that follows is puzzling. Socrates initially argues that virtue is knowledge on the grounds that virtue is good (87d) and that knowledge is the only good (87d). He then argues that virtue is not knowledge because there are no teachers and students of it (89d). Scholars typically ascribe to Socrates the view that virtue is knowledge and so this passage presents commentators with a puzzle.

When Socrates considers whether there are teachers of virtues he suggests to Anytus, who has arrived on the scene, that the sophists promise to teach the subject (91b). However, the sophists offer the kind of teaching rejected in the previous passage of the dialogue: they do not educate, in the sense of drawing out what is, in some sense, already within the learner.[29] Anytus, as we have remarked, detests the sophists and denies they teach virtue at all. Socrates stated that the claim virtue is knowledge entailed its being teachable. But since there are no teachers of virtue, it is not teachable and is therefore not knowledge. However, this conclusion is limited to the conventional teaching Meno has in mind and not learning as recollection. The passage thus raises questions about what we have in mind when we think of virtue as knowledge.

The final point that bears on this issue is Socrates' last claim, that virtue is acquired through divine dispensation (99e). This may strike a modern reader sceptical of matters divine as implausible and sketchy. However, it is worth keeping in mind our discussion of the *Ion*. There, Socrates developed an account of poetic inspiration in terms of this connection to the gods. Whatever else one might say about this claim it intimates that virtue is rare, superhuman and not the product of human effort. These qualities suggest a conception of virtue at odds with what we find in modern literature, which sometimes gives the impression that the cultivation of virtue is a relatively straightforward matter. Contrary to popular opinion, the acquisition of virtue is an achievement.

Conclusion

Socrates' main obstacle in the *Meno* appears to be wrestling with his principal interlocutor with a view to getting him to behave. One is reminded here of the people consumed with a sense of liberty in the *Republic* who refuse to be mastered and do not recognise the force of law (565d–e). The underlying point, then, in a dialogue about the acquisition of virtue, is that there are conditions a person must meet if he is to be a learner. In this respect, Meno is no student of virtue.

CHAPTER TEN

Protagoras

Introduction

The *Protagoras* enjoys a wide readership and this is hardly surprising since it deals with some of the great (and enduring) themes associated with Socrates: the nature of education and virtue; the thesis that the virtues are one; and denial of the possibility of *akrasia* (literally, a lack of strength). But it is also a widely acknowledged dramatic masterpiece. The portrait of Protagoras is even-handed and rich in detail (much of what we know of him derives from this dialogue). Socrates himself does not emerge as a clear 'hero': he plays fast and loose with his demand that the participants of the discussion stick to short questions and answers. He delivers a five-page speech on the poem of Simonides. The result is a dialogue with a vivid sense of realism.

Apart from a brief section of direct dialogue, the *Protagoras* is reported dialogue told by Socrates. Plato's irony here is his representation of a man renowned for his poor memory reproducing for his friend a lengthy discussion (more than 50 Stephanus pages). The conversation takes place in c. 433.[1] These are, then, the final years of the Golden Age of Pericles. It is, as we shall see, no coincidence that Plato should choose this point in time to conduct a discussion with Protagoras about education because he was an associate of, and gave instruction to, Pericles.

The drama

The inciting incident of the *Protagoras* is Hippocrates' arrival at Socrates' house before dawn. He learned late the previous evening that Protagoras was in Athens and he hopes Socrates will persuade the sophist to accept him as a pupil. Hippocrates' actions disclose to us the incredible excitement among the young that the new teachers provoked. He very nearly set off for Socrates' place in the middle of the night. It is hard to imagine a young person today being similarly motivated by the presence of a teacher; but substitute celebrity for teacher and we can readily appreciate their camping out all night in hope of seeing them. Interestingly, however, Hippocrates is convinced that he needs a decent reference. In the *Apology* Socrates represents the sophists as persuading the young to leave their families for a period of study (19e). But doubt is cast on this here: Protagoras might decide that Hippocrates is not a fit pupil.

Socrates is alarmed by his friend's impetuosity. While they wait for dawn to break Socrates asks Hippocrates what he hopes to gain from association with Protagoras. What unfolds strikingly anticipates the concerns fathers would later espouse regarding their sons' association with Socrates. When we purchase food or drink, we have the opportunity to consult others before we consume it; but when we purchase knowledge it is immediately absorbed into the soul. One should, in other words, be careful who one listens to.

Hippocrates' ultimate ambition is to become a sophist himself. He hesitates before admitting this, which reveals a further dimension to the drama. The sophists were already eyed with suspicion before the outbreak of the war with Sparta. Protagoras is remarkably frank about his profession, but he confirms the animosity surrounding the movement. Hippocrates, then, hopes to engage in an activity he recognises as socially deplorable. It is not insignificant that he recruits his unconventional friend to help him in this regard and not his own father.

Socrates agrees to accompany Hippocrates to Callias' house. Callias was not a sophist himself, but a millionaire who sponsored sophists. Socrates presses Protagoras to explain what a pupil will obtain through his association. The art of politics, is the reply. Here the connection between sophistry and Pericles comes to the fore.

The critical issue is precisely whether one can possess expertise in politics, the implication being that poor political decisions are the result of a lack of expertise.

The two teachers are thus pitted against one another: Socrates defends Hippocrates from Protagoras.[2] One natural way to read the dialogue is apologetically: Socrates was convicted, on one account, for being a sophist. But here we find him protecting the young from the true sophist, Protagoras.

However, this reading is not altogether persuasive. In the first place Protagoras emerges as the more decent and straightforward participant of the conversation. He tries to answer the questions he is posed honestly. It is Socrates who descends to underhand tactics, poking fun at Protagoras for speaking at length (despite his earlier following a 10-page speech) (334d). In the second place it is Socrates who provides a sophistic interpretation of the poem by Simonides. Although it's possible to interpret Socrates as parodying the sophistic method to show its inadequacy, this view is unconvincing given that Socrates uses this to preface his own line of questioning about the possibility of *akrasia*.

These points suggest that we should look at the text more carefully. The dialogue is set in the last couple of years before the outbreak of the Peloponnesian War (c. 433). The discussion takes place then at the end of the Golden Age of Athens – and of course none of the participants knows that they are on the cusp of a period of conflict from which Athens would never recover. But why does Plato choose to set this conversation with Protagoras at this point in time? Although this may simply be an historical fact, there would seem to be a more dramatic reason for choosing this moment.

Protagoras is more than the mere teacher of the young: he was, as we have already mentioned, an intimate of Pericles. Not only did they discuss theoretical questions, but Pericles appointed him to devise laws for Thurii. George Kerferd has written that the famous attacks on the sophists were thinly disguised attacks on Pericles. In the *Protagoras*, Plato presents us with *the* representative of the new learning that has impressed and shaped the intellectual life of Athens greatest leader. If Thucydides pins the blame for the fall of Athens on Alcibiades (intimate of Socrates), Plato here appears to pin the blame on Pericles (intimate of Protagoras).

The unity of virtue

In the 2004 film *Crash*, a white police officer sexually assaults a black woman under the guise of carrying out a routine body search. The next day the same officer arrives on the scene of a car accident. He crawls inside an inverted vehicle and finds the woman he assaulted. She panics, shrieks and refuses to accept his help. Petrol continues leaking from the wreck, threatening to ignite. Risking his own life, the police officer stays and persuades the woman to accept his help: he saves her life. This narrative, and indeed the entire film, drew critical comment for its portrayal of racial themes. But the episode also frames another controversy that, unsurprisingly, commanded less attention, viz. the representation of a person who apparently does both what is virtuous (an act of courage) and what is vicious (an act of sexual assault). I say unsurprisingly because we can readily imagine a person who is temperate but unjust or pious but cowardly: there is no *prima facie* contradiction in ascribing both traits to one person.

The *prima facie* absence of a contradiction casts doubt on my allegation of controversy. What, we may think, is controversial about such a representation? But when we dig a little deeper we expose tensions that threaten its coherence. In the first place we typically act with surprise when we learn that an otherwise upright individual has done something morally deplorable: a war hero, for example, who returns home and later rapes a number of women.[3] We are surprised because a single person appears wedded to the good in one situation but indifferent to, or unaware of, it in another. In fact, our surprise might tempt us to deny the person really did do something virtuous in the first place. What looked like acts of courage were, in fact, merely acts typical of a courageous person. But in his case it was not actually causally connected to courage properly so-called. This suggests that the case for an account of the virtues as wholly discrete, which would be consistent with the instantiation of one but not the other, is not entirely plausible either. So, how are we to think about the claim that the virtues are one?

The issue is vexing, not least because there is no one doctrine of the unity of the virtues. Rosalind Hursthouse recalls an unpublished paper by Timothy Campbell in which he argued there were (at least) 30 formulations of the doctrine.[4] In the scholarly literature on Plato, however, two in particular have been dominant: the unity of virtue and the unity of the virtues. The first is the view that bravery, justice, temperance and wisdom are the names for one thing: a single underlying psychological state.[5] The second is the view that a person cannot be brave without also being just, temperate and wise.[6] The challenge for the doctrine of the unity of the virtues is to give an intelligible account of the necessity of a person's being just in order to be temperate that does not imply the two virtues have something substantially in common. Plainly, the more we explain the interdependence of the virtues in terms of some common property, the more we move in the direction of the doctrine of the unity of virtue.

We have already noted that some contemporary thinkers find the idea of either unity thesis deeply implausible. But the implausibility is likely to vary with our preferred accounts of the virtues. Take, for example, Aristotle's taxonomy of the virtues, which include magnificence and wittiness. Magnificence is the virtue of spending very large sums of money on public works and public festivals. This virtue is necessarily beyond the scope of most people who are not Bill Gates. If we plug magnificence into either version of the unity thesis above, it follows that everyone who fails to be magnificent necessarily cannot be brave or just. *Mutatis mutandis* the case of wittiness: a bore is necessarily unjust and cowardly.

But the line of argument expressed in the previous paragraph is weak. In the first place, we might object to the idea that the possession of a virtue depends on external circumstances. A prisoner bound to the mast of a sinking ship is incapable of brave actions as the ship goes down, but he may well have proved a resourceful and courageous crewman in the tragedy. Similarly, a pauper could conceivably have a nose for what is fitting and tasteful in public works, despite his not having the resources to realise them. Second, and more important, the objection depends upon the truth of the account of virtues that one selects. Aristotle's preference for the virtues of the Athenian elite can be explained away in terms of his desire to flatter those in authority to avoid being prosecuted *à la* Socrates. This suggests that we must first correctly identify the true virtues before examining the possibility of their unity.

Rather than forge ahead with a defence of one or other account of the virtues, we shall conclude this section by arguing for the *prima facie* plausibility of (some version of) the view that the virtues are one. Consider, for example, the virtues of courage and temperance. The distinction between them is comprehensible: the first has to do with fear and the second with pleasure. Since these virtues regulate different emotions it's natural to regard them as discrete. But this overlooks what is involved in the regulation of any emotion.[7]

In the first place, for an individual to have the right feelings in the right circumstances he must be sensitive to various aspects of the situation. For example, a person may be in danger, and be sensitive to it, but the excessive importance he places on carnal gratification results in his staying to finish his meal while fire takes hold of the restaurant. The virtuous person, by contrast, balances these competing concerns. In the second place, emotions are ordered with respect to the right thing to do in the situation. Thus the apparently discrete areas of concern are, in virtue, regulated by practical wisdom: excellence in judging the best action to perform in the circumstances. With these points in view, we can make sense of the excellence of a diverse range of character traits. In each case, for a given area of concern, the virtuous person orders his response according to his true judgement regarding what is best. But while this explains the interdependence of the virtues, it is not clear that courage and piety, say, are absolutely identical. Interdependence does not imply identity.

The text

Since the *Protagoras* is a relatively long dialogue it will be helpful to begin by identifying the principal episodes:

- 309a–310a: direct dialogue in which Socrates praises Protagoras' complete wisdom
- 310a–314c: in which Socrates and Hippocrates discuss the wisdom of the latter's submitting himself to Protagorean instruction
- 316a–328d: in which Socrates poses two objections to the claim that the political art can be taught and in which Protagoras answers them

- 329c–334c: initial discussion of the character of the unity of the virtues
- 339a–348a: the discussion of the poem of Simonides
- 349b–351b: resumption of the discussion of the unity of the virtues
- 351c–360e: discussion of *akrasia* and implications for courage
- 361a–362a: epilogue.

Although there is conspicuous overlap between some of these topics, the connection between them may not be immediately clear. Hippocrates wants to be virtuous because he hopes to be successful in Athens. He believes virtue to be something a person acquires, and that he acquires it through instruction. If Protagoras is capable of inculcating virtue through instruction, he must know what virtue is. If he knows what virtue is, he must know whether or not the virtues are unified. The central point of tension for the unity thesis emerges between courage and knowing the right thing to do: people often know that they should face danger for the sake of what is right, but fail to do so because they are cowards. Thus the focus of the dialogue is Protagoras' claim to teach his pupils to be virtuous.

In the sections that follow, we shall concentrate on those passages that present the greatest difficulties. This inevitably will mean treating other aspects lightly and overlooking others altogether.

319a–320b

Protagoras claims he's capable of teaching young men to manage both domestic and political affairs with excellence and thereby become real powers in the state (319a). Socrates doesn't think the art of politics can be taught, and for two reasons. The first is that he believes the Athenians are wise and that when the Assembly meets to consider a building project they only listen to those who are qualified and have had good teachers (319bff.). But when they meet to discuss matters of government they listen to everybody indiscriminately. This suggests that the Athenians do not regard the art of politics an expertise. Socrates' second point is that virtuous men seldom, if ever, pass on their virtue to their offspring (319e). Such men cannot reasonably be thought to lack the inclination to inculcate virtue: the natural explanation is that the art of politics cannot be taught. Protagoras is faced with a dilemma: he must either deny that the Athenians are wise or that virtue can be taught and therefore, by extension, that he is a teacher of it.[8]

Although the points Socrates makes are superficially persuasive, they are at odds with what we learn elsewhere from Plato. Socrates maintains that the wise Athenians cannot think that the art of politics can be taught because they consult all and sundry on political matters. But we know from the *Laches* (179bff.), the *Meno* (92eff.) and the *Republic* (606eff.) that the Athenians thought that wisdom could be taught. For example, young men listen to, learned and recited passages of poetry that enshrined the shared teachings of the community.[9] This practice was pursued precisely because the Athenians believed it resulted in the production of better citizens. Socrates, then, is not straightforwardly representing the views of his fellow citizens. But he is spelling out the implication of their practice. If the art of politics is an expertise, then why is it not treated as such by men who ostensibly know? Protagoras cannot answer this question by simply pointing out that the young men of Athens do receive what is taken to be an education in virtue.

320c–328d

Protagoras answers Socrates' objections in what Vlastos describes as his 'Great Speech'.[10] The speech comprises the exposition of a myth explaining the evolution of humankind and followed by direct argument. Commentators are generally inclined to believe that the speech is a reasonably accurate representation of the form and content of Protagoras' teaching. That his speech is no straw man lends weight to this view.

The claim in question is that the Athenians are wise and do not demand to see the qualifications of anybody contributing to discussions about political matters. Protagoras explains this in terms of the universal distribution of a sense of justice among humanity (322d). Without this common ground, the state would not exist. Socrates makes a similar point himself while arguing for the provision of unity in the Ideal City (see *Republic*, e.g. 423b). Although the distribution is universal, Protagoras maintains that this sense of justice is not innate but is acquired through teaching (323c). He does not, however, argue for this claim directly (324c) but instead suggests that the view is widely shared. People do not, after all, get angry with people for faults arising from congenital defects, but they do for the execution of injustices. The phenomenon of punishment, for example, indicates that a sense of justice can be inculcated (324aff.).

With respect to the failure of great men to pass on their virtue, Protagoras makes two points. In the first place these men do try to educate their progeny (325cff.). In the second place, the variation in virtue among their sons is to be explained in terms of their aptitude for learning (327bff.). The sons of Pericles, for example, are not absolutely without a sense of justice; they are simply less competent than other young men with a great natural ability to learn. Protagoras accuses Socrates of being too 'black and white': he would prefer the company of villains, such as Eurybatus, to that of real savages devoid of any sense of justice at all.[11]

Commentators point out that Protagoras' speech meets Socrates' objections to the claim that virtue can be taught.[12] However, we might be suspicious about whether the conception of virtue operative in the speech is that which we tend to think Socrates has in mind. The threat of punishment, for example, might guide actions, but it is far from clear it makes people more just. Drivers may slow down when their satnav informs them of functioning speed cameras, but that is quite different from their having grasped the importance of driving carefully. Although their behaviour may have changed, this may not amount to the inculcation of virtue.

329c–334c

During his Great Speech Protagoras claimed that for a community of people to exist there must be something that each of its members share in common:

> If there is, and this one essential is not the art of building or forging or pottery but justice and moderation and holiness of

> life, or *to concentrate it into a single whole, manly virtue* … whoever does not respond to … instruction must be expelled from the state. (324e–325b, my emphasis)

Socrates examines Protagoras on this point:

> You said that Zeus bestowed on men justice and respect for their fellows, and again at several points in your discourse justice and self-control and holiness and the rest were mentioned as if together they made up one thing, virtue. This is the point I want you to state with more precision: is virtue a single whole and are justice and self-control and holiness parts of it, or are these latter all names for one and the same thing? (329c–d)

Socrates, then, takes for granted that virtue is one thing: what he seeks is clarification of what is meant by that claim. Neither Protagoras nor any of the other interlocutors question the assumption that virtues are one thing. The idea of the unity of the virtues was perfectly commonplace among the Athenians.[13] For Socrates, however, the idea is clearly more controversial: he thinks that we cannot straightforwardly accept that the virtue is one thing unless we are able to specify precisely what we mean.

We have distinguished two versions of the thesis that virtues are one. The first is the view that there is really just one state of the soul causally responsible for bravery, justice, piety and so on (from now on the Unity Thesis[14]). The second view is that a person cannot possess one virtue without possessing all the others (from now on the Biconditionality Thesis). But why is Socrates so concerned to identify which of these alternatives is correct? In either case, a person is either fully virtuous or not. That point, then, is not at issue. The true centre of his concern is the explanation for the necessary compresence of the virtues in any individual who can be described as virtuous in any respect. According to the Unity Thesis, the virtues are manifestations of one state of the soul. The presence of that state of the soul is, then, a sufficient condition for a person's bravery, temperance, justice and piety. According to the Bioconditionality Thesis, the virtues are discrete states of the soul. However, wisdom is necessary and sufficient for the possession of these discrete states of the soul. Having mapped out the possibilities Socrates considers, let us turn to the argument.

Socrates has asked Protagoras whether he accepts the Unity Thesis or the Biconditionality Thesis. He claims that virtue is one and that the qualities are parts of it, viz. the Biconditionality Thesis. Socrates immediately seeks further clarification:

(a) The qualities are parts as the nose, mouth, eyes and ears are parts of a face

(b) The qualities are parts like the parts of a piece of gold, which differ only from one another in terms of size, not in terms of their properties

Protagoras selects (a) and this is the subject of the *elenchus* that follows.[15] But before we consider the arguments hereabouts, we should first consider the implications of the two alternatives. Alternative (a) implies that there is no necessary connection *between* the virtues at all. After all, if one can stomach the possibility, the possession of a mouth is not a necessary condition for the possession of a nose. The possession of both a mouth and a nose is, however, necessary for the possession of a typical human face. On this alternative, virtue signifies nothing more than the possession of the full complement of virtues. It is simply the label we have for someone who, so far as excellence is concerned, is an 'all rounder'. Alternative (b), on the other hand, implies that the virtues are identical to one another: i.e. there is really only one virtue. The parts of a piece of gold enjoy all and only the same properties as each other: there is nothing to tell them apart, save for their respective sizes. On this alternative, there is, contrary to appearances, only one virtue.

Socrates develops two lines of arguments against (a) in this section: the argument from resemblance and the argument from contraries. The conclusion of the first is that justice and piety are similar; the conclusion of the second is that temperance and wisdom are the same thing. Socrates hopes to obtain Protagoras' agreement to the claim that they are similar with a view to securing the stronger claim that they are identical.

Socrates begins by drawing out the implication of (a) noted above: that, as it stands, there is no necessary connection between the respective parts of virtue (329e). Protagoras confirms this, asserting that a man can be brave and unjust. Socrates then asks whether the virtues differ from one another with respect to their functions. Protagoras confirms that this is the case: the virtues, then, do not resemble one another in themselves, nor with respect to their function (330a–b). This is the claim that Socrates targets for examination.

Socrates begins by obtaining Protagoras' agreement to the following claims:

(i) Justice is a thing
(ii) Justice itself is just
(iii) Holiness is a thing
(iv) Holiness itself is holy

Socrates proceeds to ask whether holiness is just and justice holy: he claims he himself would assent to this; Protagoras is not so sure (331b–c). The point is obviously to put pressure on Protagoras' acceptance of (a) and his rejection of (b), since resemblance tells in favour of (b) over (a). But it's worth pointing out that Protagoras could concede the conclusion that justice and holiness are very similar without being compelled to reject (a). We may be able to predicate holiness of justice, but it doesn't follow that the two are identical. However, the conclusion *is* inconsistent with Protagoras' avowed interpretation of (a): the parts of the face differ in themselves and with respect to their functions (330a–b). However, Protagoras concedes the point, quibbling about the significance of the resemblance. He does not appear to have grasped Socrates' ultimate purpose in raising the issue. Had Socrates selected courage and temperance, for example, the case for resemblance might have proved harder, though not impossible, to make.[16]

As we have already noted, the argument from contraries is more ambitious: Socrates pursues the stronger conclusion that wisdom and temperance are one thing and not two. We may set the argument out as follows:

(I) Folly is the opposite of wisdom
(II) Folly is the opposite of temperance
(III) Each thing that admits of a contrary has just one contrary
(IV) Either (III) is false or wisdom and temperance denote one thing

Since Protagoras endorses (III) (332c), Socrates infers that wisdom and temperance must be the same thing.[17] The point to concentrate on, however, is Protagoras' acceptance of (I) and (II), which only appears intelligible if we conceive of folly in the most general terms. After all, the natural opposite of temperance is intemperance, which we typically think of as a lack of self-control in matters of pleasure. The folly of intemperance lies not in the experience of pleasure but in the exposure to risk of pain and disease (353dff.). Since there are many other ways to expose oneself to pain and disease, Protagoras could claim that folly is not straightforwardly the opposite of temperance. Having said that, we know that commentators think Socrates believes virtue is knowledge. If Protagoras did try to resist (II), we can imagine Socrates explaining the pattern of thought and feeling among intemperate and unjust people in terms of their lack of knowledge of good and evil generally.

339a–347a

This lengthy section of text comprises Socrates' analysis of the poem by Simonides. There is a reasonable consensus among commentators that Socrates misinterprets the poem. If we presume, as most commentators do, that Socrates *knowingly* misinterprets the original poem, then we are forced to wonder what his purpose is. We know from elsewhere in the Platonic corpus that the sophists did, among other things, expatiate upon the poets (see, e.g. *Hippias Major* 286a–b). Some commentators argue that Socrates seeks to demonstrate in this passage the weakness of the sophistic methods: he shows that you can 'prove' anything through the exegesis of poetry, even something other than what the poem is conventionally agreed to be about. Such a reading is underscored by the caustic remarks on the practice at its conclusion: people only ever discuss poetry when they don't have any ideas of their own (347c).

This characterisation of Socrates' purpose neatly fits the origin of the discussion. Protagoras has been embarrassed and sets out to fight back against Socrates by exposing him as unable to identify a contradiction (339aff.). Since contradiction is a bad thing, the poem must be weak (339b). In this Protagoras applies standards of reasoning to poetry and so treats poetry on a par with scientific exposition. Socrates' sophistic reading, which wins Hippias' admiration, intimates the implausibility of reading poetry in this way.

But while this may be part of Socrates' purpose, scholars have speculated about other possibilities. Taylor, for example, argued that the purpose of the passage was to relax the reader's mind in preparation for the Socratic paradoxes that follow.[18] The thought here is that Plato needed a foil before he introduced some of the more controversial theses, now conventionally attributed to Socrates (that knowledge of good and evil is necessary and sufficient for virtuous deeds and actions). This assumes, though, that we know what Plato judged to be more or less controversial. None the less, Taylor's point seems right in this respect: Socrates appropriates Simonides' poem and shapes his meaning so that he appears to endorse theses Socrates will defend in the sequel to the passage. He says, for example, that 'Simonides was not so ignorant as to say that he praised all who did no evil voluntarily, as if there were any who did evil voluntarily' (345d). Simonides thus anticipates Socrates.[19]

349a–351b

Having dismissed the value of literary analysis, Socrates returns to the question of the unity of the virtues. Interestingly, Protagoras has in the meantime changed his position. Earlier he claimed that there was only a very slight resemblance between the virtues (331e). He now claims that four of the virtues resemble one another closely but that courage is different (349d; cf. 329e). With respect to this one virtue it is possible for a person to possess it and yet not possess any of the others.

Socrates challenges Protagoras by arguing that courage is knowledge, which rules out the possibility that a person could be ignorant and courageous. However, we should bear in mind that this is a stronger conclusion than he needs to defeat Protagoras. He merely claimed that courage and knowledge are not coextensive: Socrates retorts by claiming that they are identical. The argument may be set out like this:

(1) Courageous people are confident (349e)

(2) Virtue is wholly fine (*kalos*) (349e)

(3) People with relevant knowledge are more confident than those without (350a)

(4) People can be confident without knowledge (350b)

(5) Confidence without knowledge is not fine but base (350b)

So

(6) The confidence of courageous people consists in knowledge (350c)

Socrates thinks the difference between someone who is mad and someone who is courageous is that the latter acts admirably and knows what he's doing. However, Protagoras rejects Socrates' conclusion because he wishes to defend the claim that wisdom and courage are different: although all courageous people are confident, not all confident people are courageous. However, this does not block Socrates' argument, which is that confidence predicated on knowledge is courage. Protagoras proceeds to argue that Socrates has illegitimately inferred that courage is knowledge on the basis that courageous people are confident and that knowledge causes confidence. Since not all confident people are confident on the basis of knowledge, it doesn't follow courage and knowledge are one thing (350cff.). But that was not Socrates' point: he argues that knowledge is a necessary condition for the confidence displayed by the courageous; he doesn't think that all confidence is predicated on knowledge.

351b–362a

The final passage of the *Protagoras* contains the celebrated discussion of *akrasia*. This is a long and densely argued section of text.[20] Socrates' purpose in undertaking the discussion, however, is quite clear: a true account of what happens when we are mastered by pleasure will clarify the relationship between courage and the other parts of virtue (353b).[21] So although the examination of *akrasia* is intriguing in its own right, Socrates continues to pursue the question of the unity of the virtues.

Before we consider the argument, we should clarify the particular species of *akrasia* Socrates has in mind.[22] He is interested in whether knowledge is the ruling element of a person or whether actions are governed by pleasure, pain, love or frequently fear (352b–c). The point in question, then, is whether a person who knows what is good can be deflected from his pursuit of it by the passions. This person does what is evil despite his knowing what is good. Socrates and Protagoras deny this possibility (352c–d).

Socrates concentrates on the case of pleasure, though he later applies what they've learned to the case of fear, which is intuitively more relevant to the special case of courage. Most people ('the many') believe that people are overcome by pleasure. The pleasures in question are bad because they give rise to disease and poverty (353dff.). Despite their judging these activities to be bad, people are frequently overcome by pleasure and perform them against their better judgement.[23] Socrates disputes this popular explanation of the phenomenon. If we accept the present characterisation of what is going on, the only intelligible explanation is that the person in question doesn't know, or believe, that what they're doing is evil.

The many agree that they think of the good as pleasure and evil as pain (354c). They describe as evil something in which the pain outweighs the pleasure. Thus the many ascribe to people ruled by pleasure a judgement that what they propose to do will bring them greater pain than pleasure. Since they judge pain to be evil, they are further committed to judging their evil, but they undertake it for the sake of the good (355c–d). This position will be judged ridiculous. Socrates states that these people lack the art of measurement: they fail to correctly estimate the respective pleasure and pain, good and evil, of actions (357aff.). If we carry this explanation over to the case of courage we can see that the failure to act courageously is also an instance of ignorance. The person judges the avoidance of immediate pain more important than taking a stand in the face of danger. What he does not grasp is that dishonour is worse than the pain he might encounter in making a stand (359a ff.). Thus courage is knowledge of what is fearful and what is not.[24]

At the heart of Socrates' examination of the popular explanation of *akrasia* is his intellectualism: if you know what is right you do it. But underpinning this is a deeper psychological assumption regarding the relationship between beliefs and action. A vicious person's actions follow his beliefs just as much as a virtuous person's. Socrates' intellectualism wins few admirers nowadays and figures among his paradoxes. But we can dispel some of the puzzle by clarifying the case. What strikes Socrates as baffling is that a person's judgement that this is an evil thing to do could be part of the causal explanation of his performing it. That is to say, he does what is evil precisely because he judges it to be evil. When people contest Socrates' intellectualism they point to examples such as smoking. But here it is not clear that a person undertakes to smoke his cigarette because he judges it to be evil, even though he might believe it to be evil (in the sense that it may cause disease).

Socrates does not, to my mind at least, think his intellectualism is as controversial as his allegation that people do not know what is good and evil. The righteousness of our species confers upon our labours and activities a legitimacy we find difficult to resist.

Conclusion

In our survey of the *Protagoras* we have touched lightly on several aspects of the group's discussion. I noted above, however, that the core of the dialogue was Protagoras' claim to be able to teach virtue. When it comes to assessing this claim we are confronted by the problem that he conceives of his task as preparing students for the art of politics. However, although he speaks of justice and bravery, Socrates and Protagoras have not agreed on what virtue is. This, Socrates notes, should be their first task when they resume the discussion (361d). The point is carried over to the *Meno*, which starts from this very problem.

CHAPTER ELEVEN

Symposium

Introduction

The *Symposium* is a supreme dramatic and philosophical achievement that continues to command a large readership for diverse reasons.[1] The dramatic context, for instance, could hardly be more titillating: Socrates, the grandfather of philosophy, the inventor of philosophical ethics, attends an all night drinking party at which the principal topic of conversation is sex and erotic love. We, like the businessmen who ask Apollodorus to tell the story, are anxious to learn just what Socrates will say about this mysterious and complicated part of our lives. And although the guests at Agathon's party are discussing the erotic desire felt by an older for a younger man, their accounts of this desire promise potential insights of wider application.

But the *Symposium* is also of the greatest interest to students of Plato's metaphysics. The dialogue contains a remarkable description of the Form of Beauty (211aff.) that is noticeably richer than the description of the Form of the Good in the *Republic* (505eff.). The attribution of a theory of the Forms to Plato remains controversial, but commentators seeking to explore and reconstruct such a theory plumb the *Symposium* for further clues.

One of the most conspicuous features of the *Symposium* is its form. Ultimately, it is a direct dialogue between Apollodorus, one of Socrates' devotees, and a group of businessmen. That conversation takes place in c. 404, perhaps in the aftermath of the assassination of Alcibiades.[2] But the body of the dialogue comprises Apollodorus' detailed account of the drinking party at Agathon's in 416. With respect to the date of its composition, developmentalist scholars suggest it was written in the 370s, around the time of the *Phaedo* and the *Republic*.

The drama

The direct dialogue begins with Apollodorus' response to a group of unnamed businessmen who have asked him to present his account of a party that took place over a decade before. For the story to have been in circulation for that long suggests at once that it must have something going for it. But why would businessmen, of all people, care to learn about what was discussed that night and why then? One intriguing suggestion is that they are motivated by the recent assassination of Alcibiades, the famous rogue of Athenian politics. The conversation owes its origins, then, to a desire for gossip.

Apollodorus himself was an ardent follower of Socrates. He heard the story of the party from another of Socrates' disciples, Aristodemus, who had actually been at the party. Aristodemus himself hadn't been invited to the party but, at Socrates' suggestion, agrees to gatecrash. Upon his arrival he finds himself among varied company. The host of the party was Agathon, who was a burgeoning tragic playwright. His lifelong lover Pausanias was there, along with one of a new group of professional doctors, Eryximachus. Other guests included the comic playwright Aristophanes and Phaedrus, whom we know from the dialogue of that name.

A symposium was, literally, a drinking party but not quite in the sense of the contemporary drinking binge or frat party. A light meal was consumed before the observation of a series of rites that gave way to musical and sexual entertainment. But this was to be no ordinary symposium: the guests are still suffering from the hangovers incurred from the previous night's drinking. Eryximachus proposes they dedicate the evening to conversation instead of another round of carousing, his suggested topic being the praise of Eros.

One of the popular prejudices we bring to the *Symposium* is the view that the Athenians, and indeed the ancient Greeks in general, were relaxed about sexual matters. But the dialogue exposes a number of anxieties among the guests. They're keen to advertise the good that can come from the erotic desire of an older for a younger man. It bands men together; it is conducive to the development of virtue. This all sounds very noble, and then we remember that they're extolling the benefits of fellatio and sodomy.[3] While these may prove to be praiseworthy activities, it's far from obvious that their value lies in their promotion of virtue. The tenor of the early speeches, then, is euphemistic.

At the climax of the evening, just after Socrates has finished his account of his conversations with the priestess Diotima, Alcibiades bursts on to the scene. He is intoxicated and in high spirits. This is the year before the ill-fated Sicilian expedition that he pushed for in the Assembly. That would prove the turning point in the war with Sparta. He arrives consumed with the very enthusiasm that Thucydides alleges was behind the Athenian decision to undertake the campaign. Alcibiades himself is taken aback to find Socrates there and, unable to contribute a speech in praise of Eros, he instead speaks of Socrates.

While everyone else has been speaking of an older man's love of a younger, Alcibiades' tale is that of a younger man's love for an elder. He fell in love with Socrates, pursued him without success in a painful and, to his mind, exhausting affair. His ovations for sexual congress were answered with philosophical disputation. He concludes his turn by praising Socrates' arguments as the only ones in the world that make any sense.

The conclusion of speeches sees the guests reneging on their earlier agreement to drink moderately. When Aristodemus wakes he finds Socrates still up and trying to persuade Agathon and Aristophanes that anyone capable of composing a tragedy must likewise be able to compose comedy. These are two expressions of a single expertise.

Erotic love

Sex, according to Philip Larkin, was invented in 1963. Since then we have been living in increasingly sexually liberated times.[4] People now enjoy the legal protection to pursue sexual liaisons with male or female partners without fear of criminal reprisal. We are more relaxed about the presence of images of a sexual nature in film and magazines. The people in marketing cheerfully plaster photographs of stony-faced men and women in their underwear across billboards selling us cologne, perfume and (some day soon, no doubt) car insurance. We are, the world seems to say, finally at ease with this aspect of life. Problems remain, of course, but, we are given to believe, they are principally matters pertaining to the law, health or the attitudes of others. There are, for example, questions about the capacity to give consent and the need to *be responsible*. Those matters aside, the rest is simply the business of the people involved.

This familiar picture of our erotic lives, however, conceals the deepest concerns. Some of these are quite familiar. The ready availability of hard-core pornography on the internet, for example, is a worry to parents and mental health professionals involved in emotional development. There are, additionally, fears about the increasing sexualisation of young people: one UK supermarket, for instance, became the subject of intense public anxiety over the sale of padded bras designed for pre-adolescent girls. These are real worries, of course, but they reflect those matters of legality and health we have already considered. What this picture leaves untouched is the character of erotic love itself and our understanding of its significance.

The popular media give the impression that the only thing that really matters is what we get up to in our sexual encounters and how satisfactory it all was. Magazines offer patient guidance as to what your man really wants from you and how to give your woman an outstanding orgasm. But while the body and its pleasures are an obvious aspect of the phenomenon, this way of looking at matters betrays a confusion of intimacy with mere physical proximity. While people can, and do, jump into bed with one another at the drop of a hat, the popular view is that the goal is apparently the realisation of sensuous pleasure and not the achievement of an emotional union. This exposes the casualness of casual sex: nothing of overwhelming importance is at stake. A student of mine, in a seminar about Aristotle's ethics, stated bluntly that sex was 'no big deal'. That is, nothing to get worked up about. This won general agreement from his fellow students but left me wondering whether, if what he said was true, anything at all in life could count as a big deal. His remark appeared to narrow the possibilities of existence.

Erotic love has at its heart a longing for someone else. The glances and dances of courtship spin a web of meaning and significance about lovers in such a way that the most quotidian of activities becomes charming and permanent. Through this complicated pattern of interaction one's true self is steadily exposed to the other and an appreciation of theirs tenderly received and cherished. One finds in this the fullest recognition and acceptance of one's being in the world. In sex one revels in the feeling of life itself.

The remarks in the previous paragraph are apt to strike us as embarrassingly sentimental. They are, moreover, offensive. Who is to say that this is *the* nature of erotic desire? Presumably there are countless forms and this one, if it exists anywhere outside a Barbara Cartland novel, is merely one among them. The description is conceived as an attack upon freedom, upon the tolerance of the diverse forms of human intimacy. There are echoes here of a phenomenon concerning freedom of speech. Take the increasing popularity of cartoon images of Hitler on t-shirts in London. The purpose of such a t-shirt is, presumably, a test to the tolerance of others: can we, the t-shirts seem to say, tolerate the use in popular culture of light-hearted images of a mass-murdering racist? If you ask someone wearing one of these t-shirts whether they think it's offensive, he may reach for the legal protection for him to own and wear such a t-shirt. He may be right (though one wonders whether such an object would fall foul of recent legislation against the incitement to racial hatred). But the point is not whether he is breaking the law, but whether he is acting tastefully. He may have in mind the prissy and hypocritical readership of liberal newspapers, but he is, for all that, wearing an image of *Hitler* across his chest.

In the case of erotic desire, the question is not about whether two consenting adults enjoy the legal protection to pleasure one another in a mutually congenial way in the privacy of their own home. It's more that if the other person doesn't matter at all to us, or is readily substitutable, sex is reduced to an elaborate form of masturbation. The real question, then, is about a sense of taste and the enrichment of our experience through the appreciation of erotic love itself.

The text

The dialogue comprises seven speeches in praise of Eros. Although the *Symposium* is wonderfully entertaining, it's hard to imagine a comparable occasion occurring today. For the Greeks, speeches of praise (encomia) constituted a distinct literary genre. This survives today in the form of epitaphs, references and some formal occasions, such as weddings. In the comments that follow, I am greatly indebted to Allan Bloom's masterful analysis of the dialogue, which was originally part of his final work on love and friendship.

178a–180b

Phaedrus' speech makes two points. The first is that Eros is great and awesome because he is a primordial god (178b). The significance of this point is not immediately straightforward to a modern readership. But provenance and heredity were traditionally of the first importance. A person of high birth, for example, could claim possession of the excellence of his ancestors. We are, nowadays, alert to the genetic fallacy: the informal mistake of ascribing properties to something on the basis of its origins. In this case, Phaedrus argues from the primordiality of Eros to his greatness. This kind of remark was perfectly commonplace in epideictic encomia, though unlikely to persuade people nowadays.[5]

Phaedrus' second point is that Eros is responsible for one of the greatest benefits a person can enjoy, viz. 'the ability to feel shame at disgraceful behaviour and pride in good behaviour' (178c). Thus Eros is causally responsible for fine or noble (*kalos*[6]) actions. Phaedrus is principally thinking about the condition of being the object of another's affection. If I behave disgracefully, I am likely to fall in my lover's estimation. I may, then, no longer command his affections and will be spurned. My desire to remain in his cherishing regard motivates me towards what is fine and noble. Phaedrus goes so far as to say that an army composed of lovers could conquer the world (179a). He justifies the point with reference to poetic examples: Alcestis, Orpheus and Achilles (179b–180b).[7]

Phaedrus has correctly identified a dimension of our experience. In our erotic encounters we wish to be the source of our lover's arousal. We need think no further than the tired jokes (usually) about men calling out previous lovers' names in the throes of passion with new partners. He inadvertently discloses his having incorporated an image of his previous lover into his experience with his new lover. This immediately transforms the partner's experience: he is suddenly not loved; he is a mere prostitute. Phaedrus, then, calls our attention to a genuine aspect of the experience of erotic desire. This is not to say, of course, that it cannot take different forms: Jean-Paul Sartre, for example, sought to explore the modes of being-for-others and noted the distortions to which it is readily susceptible: sadism, masochism and hatred.[8] The point is simply that, though Phaedrus' speech is commonplace and pedestrian, it is not entirely without value.

The obvious objection to Phaedrus' having identified a praiseworthy feature of Eros is twofold. In the first place, Eros is only instrumentally valuable: it derives its value from its causal connection with something else we care about. In this case, we care about people doing fine things and not doing shameful things. Eros is valuable because it is alleged to make people do what is fine. But if something else, a drug for example, could bring about the same end more efficiently, say, the case for Eros is called into question. In the second place, we can readily imagine Eros producing what is shameful. I deceive a prospective lover to engineer his seduction or to remain in his cherishing regard. I am steered in these actions by my pursuit of my place in the thoughts of my lover that Phaedrus has called attention to. Pausanias picks up on this point in his speech, but develops it to different effect.

180c–185c

Phaedrus emphasised the benefits of Eros for the beloved. Pausanias speaks of the lover. He begins by asserting that nothing is good or bad in itself: its goodness depends on how it is done. This itself is a thoroughly Socratic idea. A display of endurance, for example, is neither good nor bad in itself, but good when guided by wisdom and bad when guided by ignorance. We find the idea surfacing in Aristotle, who claims that love, for example, is good when it is felt at the right time, for the reason and with regard to the right person. Pausanias applies this to the case of Eros and contends that there is a heavenly (Uranian) and a vulgar (Pandemian) form, depending on its manner.

Pausanias identifies three characteristics of the vulgar form of Eros: (i) it is sexually indiscriminate, the lover is attracted both to men and women; (ii) it is focused on the body and not the soul; and (iii) it prefers an unintelligent soul. The characteristics are clearly connected: male and female bodies may exhibit similar qualities and, since the body is the object of affection, the intelligence of the beloved is of little consequence. The object of the heavenly Eros, however, is male and intelligent: a person cannot realistically be beloved before the age of his first beard (181d). But despite his intimating this to be a noble form of Eros, Pausanias is well aware that it is widely considered immoral (183c–d): the fathers of young men prevent their liaising with older men and have them chaperoned. Their concern focuses on their sons' sexually gratifying their older lovers. It is this that Pausanias tries to defend.

He explains the origin of this concern in terms of the vulgar Eros, which is concerned with the body (182a). But it follows from Pausanias' principle that nothing is good or bad in itself, that the sexual gratification of a lover is not necessarily wrong. The challenge his defence faces is that he must justify sexual acts, which are physical, in terms of solicitude for the soul.[9] It is interesting to compare in this respect Aristotle's account of friendship, the highest form of which lives in the conversation of virtuous people whose virtue is revealed through discussion. Acts of fellatio and penetrative intercourse play no part in such an account.

Pausanias begins his defence by referring to customs and practices. In Elis it is accepted because they're not given to argument. In Persia it is forbidden as a political threat, for some of the reasons Phaedrus alluded to (viz. the cultivation of loyalty and courage). Thus Eros is respectively forbidden and admitted because of the greed or laziness of rulers. The situation in Athens, he points out, is different. There, lovers court their beloved; they woo them with poetry and philosophy. The consequence is an enduring marriage of minds, founded on the love of wisdom. This form of erotic desire is justified by its connection to noble aspirations.

The principle objection here is that the beloved emerges as a prostitute. He gratifies his lover physically for the sake of wisdom.[10] Pausanias' speech has then failed in the same respect Phaedrus' failed: the good of Eros is extrinsic. Erotic desire, for Pausanias, is simply the mechanism by which young men are educated. This line of argument will appeal to people who esteem education, but it is vulnerable to the same objection. There are, of course, other ways to educate young men. This is not to say that Eros is, after all, not praiseworthy. The point is simply that we cannot bring the matter to rest with respect to education.

185c–188e

Aristophanes is seated to the left of Pausanias but is unable to deliver his speech. He has succumbed to a bout of hiccups. He has already admitted being hungover and seeks some advice. Eryximachus, who is next to him, offers both to cure his hiccups (the joke being that the name 'Eryximachus' literally means 'hiccup fighter') and to speak in Aristophanes' place.

Pausanias tried to argue for erotic desire in terms of the soul and not the body. Eryximachus is, however, a doctor: a specialist of the body. He, recall, persuaded the party that they should refrain from drinking because it is bad for the body (176c). He argues that Eros isn't simply a state of the soul: it pervades everything in the universe. Eryximachus divides Eros in terms of the desires of the healthy part of the body and the desires of the unhealthy part of the body. The true doctor knows which desires originate from the healthy part and which should therefore be gratified.

Eryximachus' conception of Eros is entirely unerotic[11]: he states that the physician's expertise consists in his knowledge of the repletions and evacuations of the body (186c). While this does intimate penetration and withdrawal, it is otherwise generalised in such a way as to divorce a specific attraction to what is beautiful from Eros. The doctor claims to possess the science of Eros that promises to produce a healthy body and a healthy life. As we noted above, people nowadays are minded to engage in 'safe' sexual encounters. But guidance in this respect is limited simply to protecting oneself from disease and avoiding unwanted pregnancies. However, this does not tell us whether erotic desire is good or justifiable, only that its expression in action can aid or detract from self-preservation.

Eryximachus appears to think that erotic desire is pretty much inevitable (186d). The doctor's expertise is to steer a person's desires towards those things that promote health and away from those that produce disease. He doesn't further clarify his position and devotes the body of his speech to tracing the underlying principle in poetry and music. The main objection his view faces regards the credibility of health as one's supreme goal. Aristotle maintained that when people are sick their goal is health, but when they are healthy their goal is pleasure.[12] Rousseau, remarking on a parent's desire to preserve his offspring, notes that:

> You may well take precautions against his dying. He will nevertheless have to die ... It is less a question of keeping him from dying than of making him live. To live is not to breathe; it is to act; it is to make use of our organs, our senses, our faculties, of all the parts of ourselves which give us the sentiment of our existence.[13]

Eryximachus, then, has failed to provide any insights into the experience and meaning of erotic desire. It is simply something to be mastered. And we remember at this point that Eryximachus' speech has been accompanied by Aristophanes' efforts to contain his hiccups, the comedy of which cannot be captured in medical terms.

189a–193e

Aristophanes is the first of the speakers to try to describe the experience of erotic desire. He does so through a myth about the origin of the sexes. Commentators have argued that Plato does not intend us to take Aristophanes seriously, in the sense that Aristophanes himself is jesting.[14] However, even such commentators note that Aristophanes speaks more passionately than any of the previous guests and that he makes points of real tenderness. Although the speech may not be completely successful, it does justice to the experience of longing and dependency erotic desire has at its core.

In the myth there were originally three sexes: male, female and androgyne. They were all spherical, with four legs and four arms, and two sets of genitals on the outside. Human beings were judged to be powerful and threatening. Zeus undertook to limit the threat by dividing them in two. This divine wound is the source of the longing that we find in the experience of erotic desire. Aristophanes' story further captures the sense that there is just one other whom we seek: our missing half. When these divided beings began to die out Zeus pitied them and moved their genitals so that they could actually make love. The divided beings thus found temporary respite from their isolation in the throes of sexual passion.

There are two points to note here. The first is that this account explains both heterosexual and homosexual erotic desire. Where an all-male or all-female human was divided, the resulting desire is homosexual; where an androgyne was divided the resulting desire is heterosexual. This constitutes a considerable advance on the previous speakers, whose accounts are limited to homosexual love. The second point is that erotic desire itself is a desire for the pleasure of temporary union. This pleasure is transformed by the separation and represents a momentary release from our metaphysical loneliness.

Commentators who argue that Plato did not intend his readers to take Aristophanes' speech in earnest, point to the comic elements of his tale – these strange, spherical people whizzing round and then ridiculously, pitifully clinging to one another in sexual intercourse.[15] The picture is comic, but then it's not clear that sexual intercourse viewed from a certain perspective is not itself comic.[16] For all our intelligence, our alleged superiority in the natural order, we prize these occasions on which we can insert parts of our bodies inside the bodies of others.[17] The value of Aristophanes' speech is that, while he recognises the comic aspect of our enslavement to erotic desire, he nevertheless defends this preoccupation in the most touching terms.

194e–197e

Agathon begins his speech by criticising the others for having failed to speak of the god Eros at all and having instead concentrated on the respects in which human beings benefit from him. The Greek term '*kalokagathia*' literally means the beautiful and the good. Agathon ascribes this quality to Eros and thus develops his speech around his ascription of two properties: the first is that Eros is the most beautiful of the gods (195a) and the second is that Eros is virtuous (196b). In support of these contentions he adduces a broad range of evidence.

Agathon claims that Eros is beautiful (*kalos*) because he is young, tender, adaptable and of fair complexion. Eros is virtuous because he is just, temperate, courageous and wise. He concludes his speech by claiming that he tried to be both entertaining and serious (197e). This then raises a question about precisely what Agathon says in earnest and what with sincerity.

The claim that erotic desire has something to do with beauty is obviously correct. The other speakers have not touched on this point. Although both Phaedrus and Pausanias both use the word '*kalos*', they do so in its extended sense of fine or noble as opposed to its original sense of physically attractive.[18] Agathon himself claims that Eros is beautiful, a point, as we shall see, that Diotima denies in her cross-examination of Socrates. Whether or not Diotima is correct, Agathon makes an important point raising our awareness of this dimension of our experience of erotic desire.

Less convincing, however, are the claims for Eros' possession of justice, temperance, courage and wisdom. Agathon echoes Phaedrus here in his attempt to justify praise of Eros on the grounds of these qualities. But, as we mentioned above, we can readily imagine erotic desire being expressed in injustice, licentiousness and cowardice. This is the raw material for a considerable amount of art: Hollywood and pulp fiction are awash with tales of crimes of passion and corrupted desire. However, commentators argue that Agathon is actually intent on marking out a self-portrait. He is, then, ascribing these qualities to himself. This is borne out, to some extent, in his description of wisdom that has especially to do with the virtues of a poet (196e).

198a–212c

When Eryximachus proposed the guests speak in praise of Eros, Socrates claimed that he has expert knowledge of erotics (177d). This comes as something of a surprise given his famous admission of ignorance (see, e.g. *Apology*). The tension will be revealed to be more apparent than real. In erotic desire we pursue what we do not have, and this is Socrates' description of his state in the *Apology*. He recognises his lack of wisdom but he strives after it.[19]

Socrates begins his speech by cross-examining Agathon, who has been honoured with vigorous applause. While he endorses Agathon's claim that they must begin by stating what Eros is before commenting on what he does, he is curious about Agathon's views about the character of Eros. He obtains Agathon's assent to two claims. The first is that desire, and so erotic desire, is intentional: it takes an object (199d). The second point is that desire implies a deficiency: a person cannot desire what he has (200a). These points will prove central to Diotima's argument with Socrates and so it will be worthwhile considering them in greater detail.

Brentano stated that intentionality is the mark of the mental: the intentionality of states entails their mentality. Beliefs and desires are intentional. Philosophers sometimes distinguish them in terms of direction of fit. We want our beliefs to fit the world (that is, to be accurate), but we want the world to fit our desires (that is, we want our desires realised). But questions come thick and fast: is it impossible for there to be a desire that does not take an object? There is a sense in which this is correct: I can, of course, desire something that does not exist and so in that sense the object of my desire does not exist. Take, for instance, my desire for a shirt that suits me. I traipse around the shops and none does justice to the shape of my body. I wanted something but there was nothing in the world that answered to my desire. But this isn't the point philosophers are making because in this case my desire was for a shirt that suits me (= the intentional object), it's just that nothing met such a description.

The second point is that a person who possesses *x* cannot desire *x*. This may not seem straightforwardly true. After all, it can make sense to ask a person whether he wants what he has.[20] But this is a special case. A person who responded by saying 'But they're mine already' would not have understood what he had been asked, for the question requires him to imagine his standing to the object not as he presently does. He is to consider afresh whether the object motivates him towards it. Consider going through one's paperwork and evaluating whether or not to retain it. One asks oneself whether this or that is worth anything anymore. So, we can say in the central case desire for something implies deficiency. It is important to note, though, that a person may not necessarily be aware of his desire: he may only notice it the moment it is blocked.[21] We should not, then, assume that a person who desires something perceives his lack of it.

Socrates brings these two points together to contradict Agathon's contention that Eros is beautiful. If Eros is the desire for beauty then it follows, contra Agathon, that he cannot himself be beautiful. Socrates then confesses that he too made this mistake earlier in his life. He was disabused of it through his conversations with Diotima. We can divide his reported discussion with her into two sections. The first runs 201d–209e; the second 210a–212a.

In the first section Diotima makes the following points. Having argued that Eros is not beautiful, Socrates asks whether Eros is in fact ugly. Diotima points out that there is a middle ground, just as there is between knowledge and ignorance. The point of the analogy is not restricted to the possibility of an intermediary state: Eros is to be revealed as a philosopher, a seeker of knowledge (204d). Socrates objects that this claim appears inconsistent with Eros' being a god. Diotima agrees it would be inconsistent, but resolves the conflict by pointing out that Eros is not a god at all but a demon, which falls between the gods and humans.

Socrates inquires as to the origins of Eros and we learn that Eros is the offspring of poverty and resourcefulness. The description of Eros that follows is a thinly disguised portrait of Socrates himself (204bff.). The reference to his walking around without shoes confirms that we are to think of Socrates (cf. 174a). Diotima then claims that erotic desire is pretty much the desire for the whole of goodness (205d). It is thus operative in money-making, gymnastics and philosophy. This desire is possessive in character: a person seeks to possess the good. Furthermore they seek to possess it forever. At this point Diotima states that the intentional object of erotic desire is not beauty, but the bringing to birth of beauty (206e).

Let's try to bring these points together. Erotic desire is not itself beautiful and so we cannot praise it for its beauty. An erotic lover seeks what is good and this is equivalent to his wanting to bring goodness into the world. There are several aspects of this that we might want to question. In the first place, is erotic desire straightforwardly appropriative? Although people do say things like 'I want him to be mine' and certainly do feel injured by people touching their loved one, it is not immediately clear that they want to possess the person. In the fairytale 'Beauty and the Beast' the Beast in a very clear sense enjoys exclusive possession of Beauty. She's trapped in his castle and he is free to look upon her at his will.

But that is not what he needs, nor indeed what he actually wants. In the second place, the specification of the object of erotic desire is not wholly convincing. Do people in the grip of erotic desire conceive of themselves as bringing birth to beauty? That strikes the reader as a noble cause, but it's not clear this fits the psychology of people in the grip of passion.

In the second passage Diotima describes the famous 'ladder of love': a progression from our everyday conception of erotic desire to the contemplation of the Form of Beauty itself; a feat none of the guests has realised. The ladder of love comprises four rungs: physical beauty, psychic beauty, knowledge and finally the beautiful itself. An erotic lover is initially attracted to this or that particular young man, which issues in the 'birth' of beautiful ideas. But he then realises that what he loves is the beauty of the boy and thus recognises he has reason to love beauty wherever it is instantiated. The lover than ascends and comes to love the beauty of the soul over the beauty of the body. He seeks to bring to birth beautiful ideas for the improvement of the soul. This transforms him into a lover of knowledge. But the love of knowledge gives way to a love of the beautiful in knowledge and from there to the love of the Beautiful itself. The complete realisation of erotic desire culminates in the contemplation of the Form of Beauty.

Considerable scholarly attention has been devoted to this passage. It is, for example, sometimes thought that Diotima is advocating a kind of rampant promiscuity: if I want to possess, say, physical beauty and I notice that beauty is multiply physically instantiated, then I am motivated to possess as many young men as are beautiful. This certainly chimes with empirical evidence about the longevity of erotic desire and romance. But it is confounded by two points. First, the widespread sentiment that fidelity is not just praiseworthy but attractive in its own right. Second, it is not *prima facie* credible that one and the same beauty is multiply instantiated.[22] To take just one other issue, Diotima does not clearly explain the progression from one rung to the next. Precisely why should a lover of beautiful boys suddenly become charmed by the soul to the detriment of his interest in their bodies? It doesn't take much imagination to think of people effecting the generalisation between bodies without moving to prize the soul over the body.

The principle challenge, however, is the implication that the higher rungs of the ladder represent superior conditions. The lover of knowledge is better than the lover of beauty in the body. Diotima's thought is that these do not meet the specification of the intentional object of desire. What we want is to give birth to beauty: that is not fully achieved in an amorous episode. Realisation of such is the mechanism that motivates an upward search.

Socrates produces an intellectual account of erotic desire that wins unanimous applause.

214d–223d

The final speaker is Alcibiades. He arrives drunkenly on the scene in the immediate aftermath of Socrates' widely praised speech. He confesses a degree of inebriation incompatible with fine rhetoric and proposes to praise Socrates instead. His is a tale of failure. As we mentioned above, it was typical for the younger man to be pursued by the older. But here we learn that Alcibiades pursued Socrates without success.

The contrast with Diotima's teaching is striking. Whereas Diotima has spoken in terms of abstraction and generalisation, Alcibiades speaks of the particular, of Socrates. The story clearly brings pain in being recalled. Having been charmed by Socrates' revelations, Alcibiades hoped he was the object of the philosopher's affections. He thus engineers a series of failed occasions on which Socrates would have the opportunity to consummate their love.

There is, in Alciabides' speech, the counterpoint to Socrates': for him there was no substitute, for Diotima there was. Alcibiades did not ascend the ladder of love to contemplate true beauty. The question this leaves for the reader is whether Diotima's tale is at all credible.

Conclusion

The real merit of the *Symposium* is, to my mind, the fact that Plato does not appear to force our choice between these speeches. They have all developed more or less familiar dimensions of the experience of erotic love, but have equally incorporated distortions.

Concluding with Alcibiades' speech, the reader is left with a stark contrast between the profound heights of Socrates' speech and the everyday human experience of this most mysterious aspect of our lives.

NOTES

Chapter one

1 See McCabe (2006) for an illuminating discussion of the significance of the form of the dialogues.

2 Diogenes Laertius encourages this idea (III.29).

3 Although he famously states that there never will be a treatise of Plato in *Letter II*, it doesn't follow that the dialogues do not contain views that could be distilled into a treatise.

4 The thought patently does not originate with me: see, e.g. Nails (2002: xxxvii) and Beversluis (2000: ix). See also Benardete (2000), who thinks the drama indispensable for comprehension of the arguments.

5 I have subsequently found the spirit of some of these ideas in Nehamas (2000).

6 For Socrates see: Waterfield (2009) and Hughes (2010). For Plato see: Nails (2002 and 2006).

7 See Prior (2006) for an outline of the issue and Vlastos (1991) for a direct confrontation.

8 Waterfield (2009: xii).

9 I have skated over the question of whether Plato presents a unified portrait across these dialogues.

10 The meaning of Socrates' conviction remains disputable: see, e.g. Waterfield (2009).

11 See *Symposium* (215a–221b) and *Apology* (32a).

12 Bloom (1987: 274).

13 Hughes (2010: xix).

14 It's worth reading Gaita (1991: 308–30) on the moral responsibility for the scope of philosophical discussion.

15 Beversluis (2000: ix). His work contradicts this thought; he thinks the interlocutors' views are more defensible than they first appear.

16 Leo Strauss makes this observation in his idiosyncratic but very stimulating lectures on the Meno available from the Leo Strauss Center.

17 *Hippias Major*, *Hippias Minor*, *Charmides*, *Euthydemus*, *Protagoras*, *Gorgias* and *Republic* I.

18 See, e.g. Annas (1981: 8) for Plato's alleged hostility and Ahbel-Rappe (2009: 28) for a contemporary attribution of this motive to Plato.

19 Kerferd (1981: 46–9).

20 These are two grounds Kerferd considers for the public hostility towards them (1981: 25–6). The claims I attribute to Socrates can be found in *Apology* (19e and 33a).

21 Kerferd (1981: 17).

22 See Bloom (1990: 107).

23 *Pensées* (533).

24 The point is Auden's (1963: 3).

Chapter two

1 The method of question and answer itself, which is the popular conception of Socrates' method, does not appear to have originated with Socrates. See: Kerferd (1981: 32–3).

2 See Vlastos (1994: 2) and Robinson (1953; 2nd edn).

3 Brickhouse and Smith (2002: 147).

4 The terminology derives from Robinson (1953: 7).

5 For example: 'We must examine next whether it is just for me to get out of here when the Athenians have not acquitted me' (*Crito* 48b–c).

6 I follow Wolfsdorf's formulation (2003). Many scholars use 'What is F-ness?' and some, e.g. Weiss (2006), follow Robinson's 'What is X?' (1953). See Wolfsdorf (2003: 272 n.3) for the philosophical significance of these variations.

7 See, e.g. *Ion* and *Protagoras*.

8 See Young (2006) for a brief history of the word's evolution.

9 Vlastos (1994: 21).

10 The terminology derives from Benson (1987). The term 'anti-constructivism' is also used for 'non-constructivism' (e.g. McPherran (2007)). Constructivists are so-called because they think Socrates' inquiry produced significant results regarding the falsity of P.

11 Adams (1998) refers to these as hypothetical, as opposed to categorical, refutations.

12 See Kraut (1983), Wolfsdorf (2003) and Doyle (2009) for various examples of this approach.

13 Doyle (2009).

14 See Weiss (2006) for a useful discussion of the possibilities hereabouts.

15 This is Benson's 'doxastic contraint' (1987). Brickhouse and Smith (2002: 147–9) question its scope and significance.

16 Carpenter and Polansky (2002).

17 Wolfsdorf (2003).

18 These are: *Charmides*, *Euthyphro*, *Gorgias*, *Hippias Major*, *Laches*, *Lysis*, *Meno* and *Protagoras*.

19 See Santas (1979: 115–26) for a summary of pretexts for the posing of 'What is F?'.

20 See Robinson (1953: 51) and Geach (2005: 24–5). The fallacy is the product of two assumptions: (A) knowledge of what it is to be F is necessary to know you're correctly predicating F of *x*; and (B) you cannot arrive at the meaning of F by giving examples of F. Nehamas (1999: 27–58) to my mind successfully answers Geach.

21 Robinson (1953: 54).

22 Wolfsdorf underlines this point (2003: 304).

23 Robinson (1953: 57).

24 See *Early Socratic Dialogues*, (ed.) T. J. Saunders (1987: 240 n.3).

25 Anscombe (1981: 27).

26 For example: Irwin (1995: 25).

27 The terminology derives from Young (2006).

28 The standard example here is that of triangularity and trilaterality.

29 This is simply an example of a definition that does not meet the condition. It's not clear that Socrates intended this definition to specify the essence of shape. See Charles (2006: 111–14) for two distinct questions in the *Meno*.

30 See Dancy (2006: 75) for an appraisal of the plausibility of the explanatory condition.

31 Wittgenstein (1953: §66).

32 For example: *Charmides* (165b); *Laches* (186c–d); and *Meno* (70b).

33 Gulley (1968: 69).

34 Vlastos (1994: 39–66).

35 Vlastos (1991: 47–8).

36 See Irwin (1995: 27) and Cooper (2006: 178).

37 See Brickhouse and Smith (1989: 133) for elenctic warrant derived from multiple elenctic conversations.

38 Brickhouse and Smith (1994: 22).

39 Descartes (1983: 127).

40 Robinson (1953: 37). McPherran, other than Vlastos (1991) the only scholar to focus on these forms of arguments, disputes Robinson's judgement on the ground that it was based on the absence of, *inter alia*, modal quantifiers (McPherran 2007: 350). McPherran cites the example I have given as a case of inductive generalisation.

41 Robinson (1953: 35).

42 Vlastos (1991: 269–70).

43 McPherran (2007: 353)

44 McPherran (2007: 359)

45 Vlastos (1991: 29).

46 Theophrastus (2002: 52–3).

47 Robinson, e.g. thinks Socrates' irony is an instance of lying (1953: 8–9).

48 Nehemas (2000: *passim*).

49 I owe this insight to Bloom (1990: 107).

Chapter three

1 See p. 4 of this volume for a brief outline of this issue.

2 Vlastos (1971: 3–4). Taylor argues for the authenticity of *Apology* in a similar way (1926: 156–7). Our examination will not touch on the issue. See Brickhouse and Smith (1989) for a summary of the evidence.

3 Wilson (2007: 1).

4 Xenophon *Apology* (2).

5 Brickhouse and Smith (1989: 3–4).

6 Waterfield reconstructs Anytus' prosecution speech (2009: 197–200).

7 See Kerferd (1981: 21) and Waterfield (2009: 166).

8 Cited in Brickhouse and Smith (1989: 72).

9 This is Waterfield's reading of events (2009: 195–6).

10 After first drafting this section of the book I watched Professor Steven Smith's lecture on the *Apology*. He starts with precisely the same passage from Mill. He develops the point to different effect.

11 Mill (1991: 29).

12 Ibid. (1991: 20 n.1).

13 See, e.g., Burnyeat (2005: 160–1) and Hughes (2010: xix).

14 Bloom makes this point (1987: 265). It is contradicted in Libanius' *Defence of Socrates*, cited in Reeve (1989: 101–2).

15 See Martinich (2005: 21–2).

16 See Searle (1995: 117).

17 The polemical line of thought here is loosely derived from the *Republic* (537e–539a).

18 *Metaphysics* 980a 22)

19 Stokes (1992: 28) confesses that the text gets harder each time one returns to it.

20 There are, of course, alternative structures: see Reeve (1989: 3–4).

21 See Brickhouse and Smith (1989: 48–59).

22 See Reeve (1989: 5–9).

23 See Kerferd for the social need met by the sophists (1981: 15–23).

24 I use the word 'philosophy' very freely here: Socrates refers to the *elenchus*, to exhortation and self-examination.

25 It's another matter, however, whether truth-telling is always good. The story of the 'noble lie' in the *Republic*, for example, undermines the thought.

26 See, e.g. Brickhouse and Smith (1989: 63).

27 Reeve (1989: 10).

28 Against this assessment, see Brickhouse and Smith (1989: 62–8).

29 Brickhouse and Smith (1989: 62–3).

30 Against this suggestion, see Reeve (1989: 22–3).

31 McPherran raises this issue (2002: 122 n.25). It's not clear to what extent Chaerephon's rashness, nor his evident interest in the answer, bear on the reliability of his report to Socrates.

32 See Freydberg (2009) who notes how untypical it is for oracles or dreams to take the form of commands.

33 Reeve (1989: 24–6).

34 Reeve (1989: 25–8).

35 Nails (2006: 13).

36 The absence of a denial is a key element of Burnyeat's judgement of Socrates' guilt (2006). Reeve spells out the historical situation for defendants (1989: 84ff.).

37 Though presumably if he had spoken more carefully Socrates would have shifted the argument to Meletus' characterisation of the effect of his teaching as corrupting.

38 See Young (2006: 62–4) for other examples of Socrates cheating.

39 Dover (1978: 39) cited in Reeve (1989: 150).

40 See Reeve (1989: 108–9) for an account of some of the strangeness here.

41 See Metcalf (2009) for a discussion of the Socrates' comparison.

42 See Kraut (2006: 231).

43 Bloom (1987: 276).

44 Frankfurt (1971).

45 Wollheim (1984: 162). The entirely of chapter vi is pertinent to consideration of these issues.

46 Burnyeat (2005: 159).

Chapter four

1 See Popper (1995: 91ff.).

2 See *The Last Days of Socrates* (Tredennick and Tarrant, 2003: 73–7) for a brief survey of the details here.

3 Wollheim (1984: 280).

4 Forster (1951).

5 See Congleton (1974). Crito's having bribed the gaoler would seem to be clear evidence of this (43a).

6 See Anscombe (1981: 130ff.) for the exploration of this theme.

7 I will refer simply to 'the Laws' throughout. The text refers to the Laws and the common interest, which many translators render 'the state'.

8 Harte (2005: 251).

9 Zuckhert (2009: 765).

10 Versions of this conception appear elsewhere in the Platonic corpus: e.g. *Meno* (71e) and *Republic* (332aff.). See Dover (1974: 180–3) for further discussion.

11 Although not decisive, it may be a factor: Socrates tells Polus he would rather not wish to suffer wrong if he could avoid it (*Gorgias* 469b).

12 See, e.g., Brickhouse and Smith (2004: 207–8).

13 Though we can see Meno's Paradox having some bite here: how will Socrates recognise opinions that express knowledge of justice when he hears them? For Meno's Paradox see section 9.4.3.

14 See Brickhouse and Smith (2004: 221) for this point.

15 Socrates notes that this follows from the injunction that a person should do no wrong whatsoever (*Crito* 49b).

16 See Tredennick and Tarrant (2003: 224 n.25) for a discussion of the text at this point. The passage can be translated as emphasising either the manner of the agreements origination or the terms of the agreement (cf. *Crito* 52dff.).

17 Kraut (2006) and Brickhouse and Smith (2004).

18 See Bostock (2005).

19 See, e.g. Santas (1979: 11–29).

20 The existence of such a law is, on the face of it, most puzzling. It purports to protect the binding character of the law itself. But the provision for such a law suggests that the laws are not binding in their own right. This then raises the question whether the obligation to observe the law could be created by another law. After all, why should one respect that law?

21 See, e.g. Brickhouse and Smith (2004: 213–14)

22 Santas (1979: 18).

23 Santas (1979: 16).

24 Rousseau (1993: 209).

25 For further discussion of this passage, see Brickhouse and Smith (2004: 225–6).

26 Strictly speaking it is: the author of a successful petition is obliged to act in accordance with the modified directive of the Laws.

27 There are further alternatives here, such as Kraut's claim that disobedience is not wrong if one *tries*, albeit unsuccessfully, to

persuade the Laws that they're prescribing what is unjust. See Kraut (2006) and Bostock (2005) for discussion.

28 In a different sphere, we might note Paul's exhortation to the effect that we must give prayers and thanks for kings and all in authority (1 Tim. 2.1–2). He wrote this while Nero was in power and was burning Christians as lanterns in his gardens. I owe the reference to Canon Charles Stewart.

29 See Bostock (2005) and Brickhouse and Smith (2004) for further discussion of this.

30 Hume (1998: 278).

31 Santas (1979: 19–29) gives a detailed treatment of the competing interpretations.

32 I follow Brown (2006: 74) here.

33 Brown (2006) disputes the agreement I allege Socrates to have made here. Hume famously disputed the contention that residence constituted consent (1998: 283). Kraut (2006) emphasises the significance of the application for citizenship adult Athenians were required to make.

34 Bostock (2005: 217).

35 Hume (1998: 283).

Chapter five

1 See the WIN-Gallup poll: 'Global Index of Religiosity and Atheism'.

2 Aristophanes' comedy *The Clouds* parodies the phenomenon. I owe the points in this paragraph to Brickhouse and Smith (2004: 11–12).

3 See also *Protagoras* (316d–317c) and Waterfield (2009: 143–6).

4 See Dover (1974: 75–81; 133–44; 246–68) for aspects of Greek religion.

5 I use the word 'religion' here as vaguely as possible: hopefully vaguely enough to capture some aspects of the phenomenon in Athens, which differed significantly from what we might intuitively associate with religion today.

6 The New Atheists attack that way of life too, but the point is simply that both disputants need to argue for the terms of the discussion.

7 Hume (1993: 140).

8 Sharvy (1972).

9 See Hesiod's *Theogony* (126ff.; 453ff.) for these stories.

10 This passage lies at the centre of the dispute regarding the Socratic fallacy. See Geach (2005).

11 Notice Socrates' insinuation of matters independent of the gods, viz. justice and injustice, their appreciation of which is responsible for their love or hatred. This will, of course, be pertinent in the discussion of Euthyphro's third definition.

12 I follow Brickhouse and Smith (2004) here.

13 A similar point is made by Brickhouse and Smith (2004: 32).

14 See Cohen (1971) for this.

15 Cohen's characterisation of the grammatical distinction (1971).

16 See Cohen (1971).

17 See, for example, Vlastos (1991: 157–78).

Chapter six

1 See Waterfield (1987: 226) for the disappointing character of the discussion. Vlastos thought Hippias' contributions were egregious (1991: 116 n.43).

2 See Guthrie (1975: 175–6) for details.

3 Kahn (1985). Tarrant (1927) made the case against authenticity.

4 Woodruff (1982).

5 See, e.g., *Protagoras* (337c) and *Hippias Minor* (369d).

6 See Kerferd (1981: 46–9).

7 Cf. Protagoras' near identical claim (*Protagoras* 328b).

8 I owe this observation about the subject matter of the lecture to Raymond (2009: 33).

9 Woodruff, e.g. shares this interpretation (1982: 47).

10 Taylor (1926: 29, 30).

11 Kahn (1996: 118).

12 Kant (1785: 398–9).

13 Mill (1991: 159).

14 Wollheim (1993: x).

15 See Wollheim (1984: ch. vii).

16 Korsgaard (1996: 140). Just how intrusive this is depends on how we characterise obligation itself. Korsgaard makes some strong claims

about this: 'to violate [your obligations] is to lose your integrity and so your identity and to no longer be who you are' (ibid. 102).

17 Williams (1985: 174).

18 This contrast is central to Dent (1999). See Aristotle's *Nicomachean Ethics* (II.3) for the significance of pleasure in virtuous actions.

19 Waterfield (1987: 237).

20 Woodruff (1982: 47).

21 Nehamas (1999: 166–70).

22 Waterfield (1987: 227).

23 Vlastos (1994: 31).

24 Woodruff points out that Socrates is begging the question here. He would need to know the nature of fineness to know that this constitutes a counterexample. However, strictly speaking, Socrates relies on Hippias' intuitions here, though he anticipates them and does not make an assertion himself. See Woodruff (1982: 59).

25 Burke (1990: 95–9).

26 See Waterfield (1987: 249).

27 See Waterfield (1987: 253 n.2).

28 Waterfield (1987: 251).

29 See *Othello* (1.1).

30 Dover (1974: 206).

31 Waterfield (1987: 256).

Chapter seven

1 Murdoch (1977: 8).

2 Taylor (1998: 41).

3 See Shelley (1841), Janaway (1992) and Goethe (1994).

4 See Dorter (1973), LaDriere (1951), Janaway (1992) and Pappas (1989).

5 Bremer (2005).

6 An interesting exception is Apostolos Doxiadis, who is currently investigating the relationship between narrative and proof.

7 Calvino (1997), Pinter (2005) and Ackroyd (1995).

8 Mill (1859) and Murdoch (1978).

9 See, e.g. Stern-Gillet (2004).
10 Janaway (1992: 7).
11 Havelock (1963: 68).
12 Bloom (1990: 154).

Chapter eight

1 See Lane (1987: 75–6) and, e.g. Benardete (2000: 257–96).
2 See Hoerber (1968: 95ff.).
3 Kahn (1996: 149ff.).
4 Herodotus (VIII. 79).
5 Though cf. Benardete, who notes the curious limitation to the value of *hoplomachy*. Why not ask the generals what they should do with their sons outright (2000: 259)?
6 Thucydides (IV: 101).
7 This was a perfectly common ambition among Athenian citizens.
8 Hume (1777: section III).
9 See, e.g. Furedi (2006).
10 See Mental Health Foundation (2009).
11 See Falk (1982) who argues that we experience the feared object as exhibiting our lack of control.
12 Schopenhauer (1970: 134).
13 See Foot (2002: 14–15) for details.
14 See Dent (1984: 13–14) for an account of this.
15 Precisely how a love for what is right can 'win out' against fear is another deep and puzzling question. See Dent (1984) for a very cogent account.
16 See Lane (1987: 75–6) for a summary of this view and further references.
17 See Vlastos (1956: xlvii–li).
18 Kahn explores this interpretation and whether the failure of the generals to define courage implies their not being courageous (1996: 148–82).
19 See Rabbås (2004) for an intriguing account of the failure of this first definition.

20 The use of specific examples mirrors Laches's speech against *hoplomachy*, where he adduces its rejection by his favoured Spartans. Nichols (1987: 272) thinks the reliance on facts is of central importance to understanding Laches's character.

21 Lane (1987: 100 n.2 and n.3) includes references that show Plato's idiosyncratic use of texts hereabouts.

22 Cf. Dover (1974: 165–8) for typical Athenian usage.

23 Morris (2009: 620) makes a similar point.

24 The precise character of Socratic intellectualism is hard to make out (presuming, of course, Plato intended to ascribe a coherent view to Socrates). In the *Meno* (77b–78b) Socrates argues that a desire for the good is common to all humanity. Differences in our behaviour, then, owe to our judgements about what is good. But in the *Protagoras* (352bff.) Socrates appears to argue that cognitive states are (in some sense) conative states. That is to say, the judgement that *x* is good is itself motivating. See, e.g. Segvic (2006).

25 The example to consider here is the Battle of Thermopylae. See Herodotus (VII: 201ff.).

26 Thucydides (VII. 50).

27 Santas puts the point in these terms (1979: 450).

28 Santas formalises the entire passage and argues it's fallacious (1979: 457ff.).

Chapter nine

1 Cf. the poets and the rhapsodes in *Ion* and *Apology*.

2 This is Leo Strauss's reading of Meno's purpose. My appreciation of the drama owes much to the audio recordings of his lectures on *Meno*, which are available at the Leo Strauss Center.

3 Taylor (1926: 130) stresses this point.

4 Klein (1965: 38)

5 Strauss stresses this point in his lectures (op. cit.).

6 Schopenhauer (1970: 90).

7 Cf. Nietzsche, who thought that the origin of human conscience was written in blood (1887: II:3).

8 Rousseau (1979: 101).

9 Rousseau himself was perfectly aware of the fact.

10 See, e.g., Karasmanis (2006: 129).

11 Dancy (2006: 81).

12 Socrates characterises this as a species of flattery. See *Gorgias* (463a–b).

13 See, e.g. Crombie (1994: 188).

14 Crombie (1994: 188).

15 Charles (2006).

16 Crombie (1994: 192).

17 See Irwin (1995: 129) for the contrast developed here.

18 I owe this point to Strauss (op. cit.).

19 See Nakhinikian (1994) and Brickhouse and Smith (2006) for discussion.

20 Nehamas (1994: 221).

21 See p. 42 for a brief discussion of eristic.

22 White (1994: 152).

23 Socrates reformulates the paradox and subtly changes it, dropping (ii) here. Nehamas (1994) endorses White's contention that nothing substantially rests on this. For discussion, see Scott (2006: 77–9).

24 See Scott (2006) for Meno's laziness.

25 White (1994: 163–4).

26 White (1994: 155–7).

27 See, e.g., Scott (2006: 100–1).

28 Scott (2006: 121) treats this comment more cautiously than I have here.

29 The different teachers in this passage are noted by Irwin (1995: 140–1).

Chapter ten

1 Although Wolfsdorf (1997) claims the conversation takes place during the first decade of the Pelopponesian War, he argues that the anachronisms present in the dialogue forbid any greater specificity.

2 Nussbaum (1986: 119).

3 Hursthouse (1999: 155).

4 Hursthouse (1999: 153 n.9).

5 This is Penner's position (1973).

6 This is Vlastos's position.

7 I have referred here to emotion for the sake of continuity with the cases of courage and temperance. There are other virtues, such as generosity, that are more intuitively thought of in terms of action, but I do not touch on the point in the text.

8 Kerferd frames the matter in these terms (1981: 133).

9 See Chapter Seven for the development of this theme in the *Ion*.

10 Vlastos (1956).

11 This point enshrines Protagoras' relativism. For a discussion of Protagoras' views in Plato see Kerferd (1981: 83–110).

12 See, e.g. Guthrie (1956: 31). See also Nussbaum for an assessment of Protagoras' thinking (1986: 100–6).

13 Annas (1993: 73).

14 I take these labels from Vlastos (1981: 224). Vlastos frames the development of the argument very differently from the presentation here.

15 Vlastos (1981: 225) thinks both (a) and (b) are interpretations of the Biconditionality Thesis. He does not treat (b) as an expression of the Unity Thesis.

16 In the *Laches* Socrates suggests that people show courage in being temperate (191d–c). But this is not obviously intuitive to the modern reader.

17 Vlastos (1981: 246) interprets this passage as claiming that wisdom and temperance are members of one class, the opposite of which class is folly.

18 Taylor (1926: 215).

19 See Carson (1992) both for discussion and for a reconstruction of Simonides' poem.

20 See Santas (1979: 195–217) for a detailed analysis of the entire passage.

21 Although Socrates speaks of parts here, he is speaking to Protagoras' conception of the matter and is not asserting his own view.

22 See Matthews (1966) for a taxonomy of positions hereabouts.

23 Holton distinguishes this phenomenon from weakness of will (2009: 70–96).

24 The argument here is held to contradict the argument of the *Laches* (194cff.). See Devereux (2006) for discussion.

Chapter eleven

1 I follow Nehamas here (1999: 303).

2 The suggestion is Nussbaum's. See her (1986: 169–71).

3 Bloom (2001: 79–86).

4 This line of thought owes much to Bloom (1987: 97–108).

5 Taylor (1926: 213).

6 For the significance of the *kalon* see section 6.3.

7 Bloom questions the suitability of these examples for the point Phaedrus hopes to make: Alcestis, for example, is a woman, whereas Phaedrus emphasises manly virtue (2001: 82–3).

8 Sartre (1995: 364–430).

9 Bloom (2001: 87).

10 Bloom (2001: 92).

11 Bloom (2001: 99).

12 *Nicomachean Ethics* (1095a 22–6).

13 Rousseau (1979: 42).

14 Taylor (1926: 219).

15 Taylor (1926) does not attempt to reconcile the two elements as I have here.

16 Nussbaum (1986: 172) emphasises this point.

17 Nussbaum (1986: 172).

18 Bloom stresses this (2001: 115).

19 I have presented Bloom's interpretation here (2001: 130). Reeve (2006) offers an alternative reading: Socrates is making a pun. 'Eros' is erotic love; 'erotan' is the asking of questions. Thus, for Reeve, Socrates is stating that he has knowledge of asking questions, which is tantamount to his elenctic practice.

20 Price (1989: 19).

21 Wollheim (1999: 18).

22 Nussbaum (1984: 180).

GUIDE TO FURTHER READING

Works by Plato in translation

Complete Works J. M. Cooper (ed.) (USA: Hackett, 1997)
Early Socratic Dialogues T. J. Saunders (ed.) (UK: Penguin, 1987)
The Last Days of Socrates trans. H. Tredennick and H. Tarrant (UK: Penguin, 2003)
Protagoras and Meno trans. W. K. C. Guthrie (UK: Penguin, 1956)
Republic trans. D. Lee (UK: Penguin, 1987)
Symposium trans. S. Benardete (USA: University of Chicago, 2001)
Symposium trans. R. Waterfield (UK: Oxford University Press, 1994)
Lysis, Symposium, Gorgias trans. W. R. M. Lamb (UK: Harvard, 2001)
Laches, Protagoras, Meno, Euthydemus trans. W. R. M. Lamb (Michigan: Harvard, 2006)
Statesman, Philebus, Ion trans. H. N. Fowler and W. R. M. Lamb (UK: Harvard, 2001)
Euthyphro, Apology, Crito, Phaedo, Phaedrus trans. H. N. Fowler (USA: Harvard, 1914)

Commentaries

Brickhouse, T. C. and Smith, N. D. *Socrates on Trial* (UK: Oxford University Press, 1989)
—*Plato and the Trial of Socrates* (UK: Routledge, 2004)
Guthrie, W. K. C. *Plato: the man and his dialogues: earlier period* (UK: Cambridge University Press, 1975)
Reeve, C. D. C. *Socrates in the Apology* (USA: Hackett, 1989)
Scott, D. *Plato's Meno* (UK: Cambridge University Press, 2006)
Taylor, A. E. *Plato: The Man and His Work* (USA: Dover, 1926)

Collections of articles

Ahbel-Rappe, S. and Kamtekar, R. (eds) *A Companion to Socrates* (Singapore: Wiley-Blackwell, 2006)

Benson, H. (ed.) *A Companion to Plato* (Singapore: Wiley-Blackwell, 2006)

Day, J. (ed.) *Plato's Meno in Focus* (UK: Routledge, 1994)

Judson, L. and Karasmanis, V. (eds) *Remembering Socrates* (UK: Oxford University Press, 2006)

Kamtekar, R. (ed.) *Plato's Euthyphro, Apology and Crito* (USA: Rowman and Littlefield, 2005)

Works otherwise referred to

Ackroyd, P. 'Fact and Literary Fiction' in *The Waterstone's Magazine* (1995)

Adams, D. '*Elenchus* and Evidence' in *Ancient Philosophy* 18 (1998)

Ahbel-Rappe, S. *Socrates: A Guide for the Perplexed* (UK: Continuum, 2009)

Annas, J. *An Introduction to Plato's* Republic (UK: Oxford University Press, 1981)

—*The Morality of Happiness* (Oxford: Oxford University Press, 1993)

Anscombe, G. E. 'The Source of the Authority of the State' in *Ethics, Religion and Politics* (UK: Blackwell, 1981)

Aristophanes *The Clouds* (any edition)

Auden, W. H. *The Dyer's Hand* (UK: Faber, 1963)

Benardete, S. *The Argument of the Action* (USA: University of Chicago, 2000)

Benson, H. 'The Problem of the *Elenchus* Reconsidered' in *Ancient Philosophy* 7 (1987)

Beversluis, J. *Cross-Examining Socrates: A Defence of the Interlocutors in Plato's Earlier Dialogues* (USA: Cambridge University Press, 2000)

Bloom, A. *The Closing of the American Mind* (USA: Simon and Schuster, 1987)

—*Giants and Dwarfs* (USA, Touchstone, 1990)

—'The Ladder of Love' in Benardete (2000)

Bostock, D. 'The Interpretation of Plato's *Crito*' in Kamtekar (2005)

Bremer, J. *Plato's Ion* (USA: Bibal Press, 2005)

Brickhouse, T. C. and Smith, N. D. *Plato's Socrates* (USA: OUP, 1994)

—'The Socratic *Elenchus*?' in Scott, G. (ed.) *Does Socrates have a Method?* (USA: Pennsylvania State University Press, 2002)

—'The Socratic Paradoxes' in Benson (2006)
Brown, L. 'Did Socrates Agree to Obey the Laws of Athens?' in Judson and Karasmanis (2006)
Burke, E. *A Philosophical Inquiry into Our Ideas of the Sublime and Beautiful* (UK: Oxford University Press, [1757] 1990)
Burnyeat, M. 'The Impiety of Socrates' in Kamtekar (2006)
Calvino, I. 'Philosophy and Literature' (1971) reprinted in *The Literature Machine* (UK: Vintage, 1997)
Carpenter, M. and Polansky, R. 'The Variety of Elenchi' in Scott, G. (ed.) *Does Socrates have a Method?* (USA: Pennsylvania State University Press, 2002)
Carson, A. 'How not to read a poem: unmixing Simonides from *Protagoras*' in *Classical Philology* 87 (1992)
Charles, D. 'Types of Definition in the *Meno*' in Judson and Karasmanis (2006)
Cohen, S. 'Socrates on the Definition of Piety: *Euthyphro* 10a–11b' in *Journal of the History of Philosophy* 9 (1971)
Congleton, A. 'Two Kinds of Lawlessness in Plato's Crito' in *Political Theory* 2 (1974)
Crombie, I. 'Socratic Definition' in Day (1994)
Dancy, R. M. 'Platonic Definitions and Forms' in Benson (2006)
Dennett, D. C. *Breaking the Spell* (UK: Penguin, 2006)
Dent, N. J. H. *The Moral Psychology of the Virtues* (UK: Cambridge University Press, 1984)
—'Virtue, eudaimonia and teleological Ethics' in Carr, D. (ed.) *Virtue Ethics and Moral Education* (UK: Routledge, 1999)
Descartes, R. *The Essential Descartes* (USA: New American Library, 1983)
Devereux, D. 'The Unity of the Virtues' in Benson (2006)
Dorter, K. 'The *Ion*: Plato's Characterisation of Art' in *Journal of Aesthetics and Art Criticism* 32 (1973)
Dover, K. J. *Greek Popular Morality* (USA: Hackett, 1974)
Doyle, J. 'The Socratic Elenchus: No Problem' in Smiley, T. J., Lear, J. and Oliver, A. (eds) *The Force of Argument* (UK: Routledge, 2009)
Falk, B. 'What are we frightened of?' in *Inquiry* 25 (1982)
Foot, P. *Virtues and Vices* (USA: Oxford University Press, 2002)
Forster, E. M. *Two Cheers for Democracy* (USA: Harcourt, 1951)
Frankfurt, H. 'Freedom of the Will and the Concept of a Person' in *Journal of Philosophy* 68 (1971)
Freydberg, B. 'Oracles and Dreams Commanding Socrates' in Fragan, P. and Russon, J. (eds) *Re-examining Socrates in the* Apology (USA: Northwestern University Press, 2009)
Furedi, F. *Culture of Fear Revisted* (UK: Continuum, 2006)

Gaita, R. *Good and Evil* (UK: Routledge, 1991)
Geach, P. 'Plato's Euthyphro: Analysis and Commentary' in Kamtekar, (2005) originally in *The Monist* 50 (1966)
Goethe, J. W. 'Plato as Party to Christian Revelation' in Gearey, J. (ed.) *Collected Works: Essays on Art and Literature* vol. 3 (USA: Princeton, [1826] 1994)
Gulley, N. *The Philosophy of Socrates* (UK: Macmillan, 1968)
Harte, V. 'Conflicting Values in Plato's *Crito*' in Kamtekar (2005)
Havelock, E. *Preface to Plato* (USA: Harvard, 1963)
Herodotus *Histories* trans. R. Waterfield (UK: Oxford University Press, 1998)
Hesiod *Theogony* (any edition)
Hoerber, R. G. 'Plato's *Laches*' in *Classical Philology* 63 (1968)
Holton, R. *Willing, Wanting, Waiting* (UK: Oxford University Press, 2009)
Hughes, B. *The Hemlock Cup* (UK: Cape, 2010)
Hume, D. *An Enquiry Concerning the Principles of Morals* (any edition, 1777)
—*Dialogues Concerning Natural Religion and the Natural History of Religion* (UK: Oxford University Press, 1993)
—*Selected Essays* (UK: Oxford University Press, 1998)
Hursthouse, R. *On Virtue Ethics* (UK: Oxford University Press, 1999)
Irwin, T. *Plato's Ethics* (USA: Oxford University Press, 1995)
Janaway, C. 'Craft and Fineness in *Ion*' in *Oxford Studies in Ancient Philosophy* X (1992)
Kahn, C. 'The Beautiful and the Genuine' in *Oxford Studies in Ancient Philosophy* III (1985)
—*Plato and the Socratic Dialogue* (UK: Cambridge University Press, 1996)
Kant, I. *Groundwork of the Metaphysic of Morals* (any edition, 1785)
Karasmanis, V. 'Definition in Plato's *Meno*' in Judson and Karasmanis (2006)
Kerferd, G. *The Sophistic Movement* (1981)
Klein, J. *Plato's Meno* (1965)
Korsgaard, C. *The Sources of Normativity* (UK: Cambridge University Press, 1996)
Kraut, R. 'Comment on Gregory Vlastos, "The Socratic *Elenchus*"' in *Oxford Studies in Ancient Philosophy* I (1983)
—'*Dokimasia*, Satisfaction and Agreement' in Kamtekar (2006)
LaDriere, C. 'The Problem of Plato's *Ion*' in *Journal of Aesthetics and Art Criticism* 10 (1951)
Lane, I. 'Introduction' and 'Notes' in Saunders (1987)
McCabe, M. M. 'Form and the Platonic Dialogues' in Benson (2006)

McPherran, M. 'Justice and Pollution in *Apology*' in *Apeiron* 35 (2002)
—'Socratic Epagoge and Socratic Induction' in *Journal of the History of Philosophy* 21 (2007)
Martinich, A. P. *Hobbes* (UK: Routledge, 2005)
Matthews, G. 'Weakness of Will' in *Mind* 75 (1966)
Mental Health Foundation *In the Face of Fear* (2009)
Metcalf, R. 'Socrates and Achilles' in Fragan, P. and Russon, J. (eds) *Re-examining Socrates in the* Apology (USA: Northwestern University Press, 2009)
Mill, J.-S. 'Thoughts on Poetry and Its Varieties' in *Dissertations and Discussions* (1859)
—*On Liberty* (UK: Oxford University Press, 1991)
Morris, T. F. 'Manliness in Plato's *Laches*' in *Dialogue* 48 (2009)
Murdoch, I. *The Fire and the Sun* (UK: Oxford University Press, 1977)
—'Philosophy and Literature' in Magee, B. (ed.) *Talking Philosophy* (UK: Oxford University Press, 1978)
Nails, D. *The People of Plato* (USA: Hackett, 2002)
—'The Life of Plato of Athens' in Benson (2006)
Nakhnikian, G. 'The First Socratic Paradox' in Day (1994)
Nehamas, A. 'Meno's paradox and Socrates as a teacher' in Day (1994)
—*Virtues of Authenticity* (USA: Princeton, 1999)
—*The Art of Living* (USA: University of California, 2000)
Nichols, J. H. 'Introduction to the *Laches*' in Pangle, T. L. *The Roots of Political Philosophy* (USA: Cornell University Press, 1987)
Nussbaum, M. *The Fragility of Goodness* (USA: Cambridge University Press, 1986)
Pappas, N. 'Plato's *Ion*: The Problem of the Author' in *Philosophy* 64 (1989)
Pascal, B. *Pensées* (any edition)
Penner, T. 'The Unity of Virtue' in *Philosophical Review* (1973)
Pinter, H. 'Art, Truth and Politics: The Nobel Lecture' in *Publications of the Modern Language Association* (2005)
Popper, K. *The Open Society and Its Enemies* vol. 1 (UK: Routledge, 1995)
Price, A. *Love and Friendship in Plato and Aristotle* (UK: Oxford University Press, 1989)
Prior, W. 'The Socratic Problem' in Benson (2006)
Rabbås, Ø. 'Definitions and Paradigms: Laches' First Definition' in *Phronesis* 49 (2004)
Raymond, C. 'The *Hippias Major* and Aesthetics' in *Literature and Aesthetics* 19 (2009)
Reeve, C. D. C. 'Plato on Eros and Friendship' in Benson (2006)
Robinson, R. *Plato's Earlier Dialectic* (UK: Oxford University Press, 1953)

Rousseau, J.-J. *Emile, or on Education* (USA: Basic Books, 1979)
—*The Social Contract, and The Discourses* (UK: J. M. Dent, 1993)
—*Julie or The New Heloise* (USA: Dartmouth, 1997)
Santas, G. *Socrates* (UK: Routledge, 1979)
Sartre, J.-P. *Being and Nothingness* (UK: Routledge, 1995)
Schopenhauer, A. *The World as Will and Representation* vol. II (USA: Dover, 1958)
—*Essays and Aphorisms* (UK: Penguin, 1970)
Searle, J. R. *The Construction of Social Reality* (UK: Penguin, 1995)
Segvic, H. 'No One Errs Willingly' in Ahbel-Rappe and Kamtekar (2006)
Sharvy, R. '*Euthyphro* 9b–11b: Analysis and Definition in Plato and Others' in *Nous* 6 (1972)
Shelley, P. 'A Defence of Poetry' in *Essays, Letters from Abroad, Translations and Fragments* (UK: Bradbury and Evans, 1841)
Stern-Gillet, S. 'On (mis)interpreting Plato's *Ion*' in *Phronesis* 49 (2004)
Stokes, M. 'Socrates' Mission' in Gower, S. and Stokes, M. (eds) *Socratic Questions* (UK: Routledge, 1992)
Tarrant, D. 'The Authorship of the *Hippias Major*' in *Classical Quarterly* 21 (1927)
Taylor, C. C. W. *Socrates* (UK: Oxford University Press, 1998)
Thucydides *A History of the Peloponnesian War* trans. T. Hobbes
Vlastos, G. (ed.) Plato: *Protagoras* (USA: Liberal Arts Press, 1956)
—'The Paradox of Socrates' in *The Philosophy of Socrates* (USA: Anchor Books, 1971)
—'The Unity of the Virtues in the *Protagoras*' in Vlastos, G. (ed.) *Platonic Studies* (USA: Princeton, 1981)
—*Socrates* (UK: Cambridge University Press, 1991)
—*Socratic Studies* (UK: Cambridge University Press, 1994)
Waterfield, R. 'Introduction' and 'Notes' in Saunders (1987)
—*Why Socrates Died* (UK: Faber, 2009)
Weiss, R. 'Socrates: Seeker or Preacher?' in Ahbel-Rappe and Kamtekar (2006)
White, N. P. 'Inquiry' in Day (1994)
Wilde, O. *The Complete Letters* (UK: Fourth Estate, 2000)
Williams, B. *Ethics and the Limits of Philosophy* (UK: Fontana, 1985)
Wilson, E. *The Death of Socrates* (UK: Profile, 2007)
Wittgenstein, L. *Philosophical Investigations* (UK: Blackwell, 1953)
—*Culture and Value* (UK: Blackwell, 1980)
Wolfsdorf, D. 'The Dramatic Date of Plato's Protagoras' in *Rheinisches Museum für Philologie* 140 (1997)
—'Socrates' Pursuit of Definitions' in *Phronesis* 48 (2003)
Wollheim, R. *The Thread of Life* (USA: Cambridge University Press, 1984)

—*The Mind and Its Depths* (USA: Harvard, 1993)
—*On the Emotions* (UK: Yale, 1999)
Woodruff, P. *Hippias Major* (USA: Hackett, 1982)
Young, C. 'The Socratic *Elenchus*' in Benson (2006)
Zuckhert, C. *Plato's Philosophers* (USA: University of Chicago, 2009)

INDEX